# BUTTON BUTTON

## identification and price guide

### Peggy Ann Osborne

*Schiffer Publishing Ltd*

77 Lower Valley Road, Atglen, PA 19310

## ACKNOWLEDGEMENTS

I'd like to "give a hand" to those collectors and friends who have so generously loaned buttons for this book—Mary Louise VandeBerg, Marion Roche, Ann Wilson, M.W. Speights, Florence Dieckmann, and Sandra Dieckmann.

Thank you also to the businesses that extended their hands and shared both buttons and information: David Rector (Blue Moon); Daniel Baughman (for Battersea, Ltd., Bergamot Brass Works); Will Stokes (Blue Flame Studios); Judi Danforth and Peggy Zilinsky (Danforth Pewterers); Drucilla White (Duttons for Buttons); Robert Prenner (Ben Silver); Glenna Bennett (J.H.B. International); Pat Molnar (Buttons & Things); Mr. Freitag (B. Blumenthal & Co., Ltd.); Björn Amelan (for Patrick Kelly); David Schoenfarber (Streamline Industries, Inc.); Debra Hill (Britex Fabrics); Judy Snow (Bygone Buttonwear); and Dan Farber (Fishman's Fabrics).

And to the people who gave me their priceless knowledge and enthusiasm—you, too, had a hand in this book: Sam Gassman; Barbara Johnson; Lucille Weingarten; Tessie Yustak; Joyce Lowry; Sally Luscomb; Lois Calkins; Carol Freitag; Jean Speights; Claire Garrity; Robert Selman; George Theofiles (The Miscellaneous Man); Florence Bubser; Christine Harrison; and especially the editor of the **National Button Bulletin**, M.W. (Freddie) Speights, for his friendship, advice, and his own amazing research.

Finally, I'd like to thank my parents—Les and Mary Louise VandeBerg for their unending patience, and assistance, and Peter and Nancy Schiffer for more than I could ever acknowledge or repay.

Revised Price Guide 1997

Copyright © 1993, 1997 by Peggy Ann Osborne.
Library of Congress Catalog Number: 92-63104.

ISBN: 0-7643-0082-2
Printed in Hong Kong

Published by Schiffer Publishing, Ltd.
77 Lower Valley Road
Atglen, PA 19310
Phone: (610) 593-1777
Fax: (610) 593-2002
Please write for a free catalog.
This book may be purchased from the publisher.
Please include $2.95 for shipping.
Try your bookstore first.

We are interested in hearing from authors
with book ideas on related subjects.

Fun and games! Modern buttons (ca. 1935-1975) relating to parlor games: chess, Scrabble®, dice, cards, bingo, tic-tac-toe, and roulette.

**DEDICATION**

To John for understanding
and to Lynne Speaker for inspiration.

# Contents

# Introduction

We are in a time and culture that takes buttons for granted. Even the word *button* is ambiguous: if you mention that you collect buttons, most people assume you mean pin-backs. After explaining that you are talking about *clothing buttons...real buttons...button-buttons...* you normally get only a blank stare, sometimes followed by a nearly imperceptible half-step backwards and a raised eyebrow.

I think it's fun to show a non-collector some of the buttons from the past: while they look at the buttons, I look at them. It's fascinating to see just how amazed they are at the sight of buttons with beautiful pictures or funny subjects or those made from precious materials. Their amazement often turns to disbelief, "But these weren't really buttons, I mean, no one actually wore them?!" And after the usual assurances and explanations (that button collectors have all gotten used to giving,) they either shrug their shoulders and dismiss the whole field with a shake of their head, or they begin to see the artistry and admire the workmanship that went into—what had once seemed to them—a rather inconsequential item. It's then that a new button collector is born.

It was this amazement and wonder that I felt when I saw an interesting old button for the first time, and before I knew it, I was hooked. Actually, the button that first intrigued me was one that I would now find pretty mundane, but it was light years ahead of the plain ones that I was used to.

Buttons are addictive. You can become totally immersed in them. For me, they've been a journey through the world, an excursion into history, and an art appreciation course. Buttons can lead to a study of almost any subject you can think of. Some people collect only the buttons that relate to their other interests: paperweight collectors collect tiny paperweight buttons, golfers collect golfing designs, dog lovers collect dog buttons, bird watchers try to

A mere ½" in diameter, this is a good example of the fine workmanship found on many nineteenth-century buttons. Ornately carved, the hollow wooden button contains a background disc of iridescent-blue abalone pearl which contrasts with the mother-of-pearl carved cameo dog attached above it with two, faceted cut-steel rivets.

Another example of complex workmanship in a small button from the past, the natural horn was first compression molded to change its surface contour and four faceted cut-steel rivets were fixed into the raised area, strictly for decor. Tiny mother-of-pearl flowers were inlaid petal by petal, hand-painted with minute red lines, and finally, the finishing touches were painted in gold.

Table-tennis buttons (and a shuttlecock button made of Bakelite and cork) belonging not to a button collector, but a sports fan. *Courtesy of an anonymous Ping-Pong © fanatic.*

find every species of bird on buttons, opera buffs collect buttons with scenes from famous operas, and so on. Then there are those who collect them all.

The best sources for old buttons are the numerous button dealers throughout the United States and the United Kingdom. There are even specialized shops that carry nothing but buttons, old and new, in Chicago, New York, London, and Paris.

Other sources are general antiques shops and flea markets. Most antiques dealers fall into one of two categories: those who know about button collecting, but nothing about prices, (and so, afraid of being "taken", charge way more than a button dealer would) and those who know absolutely nothing about button collecting (and wonder why you have no interest in buying their quart jar of junk buttons for $5.00.) Still, you can get lucky, so by all means, do look for buttons at markets and shows. (There has been such an increase in the collecting of buttons in recent years that many more general dealers now are selling them.)

Don't overlook neighbors, relatives, and friends with old family button boxes. Until this generation, every home had one. Some will contain surprisingly good buttons. The recycling of buttons was far more prevalent in days gone by than may be realized.

When I began collecting, I ruined many of my earliest metal buttons by trying to clean them with water. Although I was certain that I'd dried them thoroughly, I didn't understand the inner construction of the buttons and

Just Ducky! An assortment of duck buttons decorates a t-shirt owned by Chicago's famed "Cold Duck," a non-button collector who is said to have quacked-up from sewing them all on. *Courtesy Sandra Dieckmann collection.*

they soon rusted. One-piece metal buttons of silver, copper, and brass can be polished, but steel and iron buttons will rust (these are magnetic if you need to identify them) and tin is harmed as well. Many metal buttons dating from the 1880s to 1915 have brass fronts and painted tin backs with cardboard in between to absorb moisture. If water gets in, the cardboard will stay wet, eventually causing the interior, back, and shank to rust. It's best to leave them alone or polish them with a gentle commercial paste that needs no rinsing.

Many buttons, especially those made of mother-of-pearl or metal, will benefit from a good buffing with a dry terry towel. (Don't buff painted examples or those with fragile decor.) One-piece molded-glass buttons (undecorated ones, with no steel trim or painted areas) can be gently washed. Glass with a metal back or mounting, or with glued sections, cannot get wet. Cleaning buttons is mostly a matter of common sense: when in doubt, don't; and if you do, be very conservative.

If you love the look of certain buttons and want to use them on clothing, go ahead, but again, be sensible. Solid cast metals are fine to use, as are solid glass ones; Bakelite and some of the hard plastics are pretty indestructible, but painted trim may wear off. Celluloid buttons will disappear into thin air at the touch of an iron, and don't put them in the clothes dryer, either! You can attach buttons that you want to remove quickly for laundering, or just to switch the look, by using little safety pins behind the fabric, through the shank, and back under the fabric. There are specially-designed little pins (called button pins) sold for this very purpose at fabric shops.

Enjoy your buttons, whether you collect them seriously, just for fun, or just to wear. Many non-collectors are now buying decorative or thematic buttons to sew onto clothes, hats, vests, and so forth.

I urge you to join a button club or organization. The shared knowledge and friendships add tremendously to your own enthusiasm. The larger state and national organizations usually publish very informative magazines for their members, and these are irreplaceable resources for information (and ads).

If I could make a wish for experienced collectors, it would be that they could always see their buttons through the eyes of the newcomer. We tend to get involved with values and rarities and specializations, and pass right by the beauty and complexity of many buttons we would have once marvelled at, simply because they're not as posh as those we've gotten since.

And to the would-be collector just starting out, I wish you the joy and friendships that buttoning can bring, and the hope that you never lose sight of what drew you to buttons in the first place—the workmanship, regardless of relative value or rarity; the incredible detail; and the amazing artistry and balance achieved on so small a canvas.

American button collectors first banded together in 1938 with the organization of the National Button Society. Most collectors also belong to a state club and one or more local chapters. The N.B.S. publishes a wonderfully informative magazine, one of the benefits of membership. Many state clubs also publish their own bulletins.

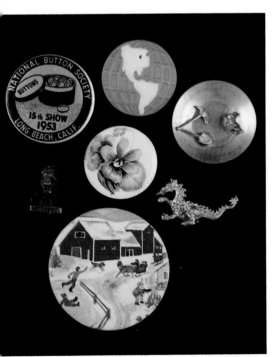

It has become customary for State and National button clubs to give a favor button to those attending annual conventions. Sometimes designed by the host club members themselves, others are custom-ordered from button companies or artists. Usually backmarked and dated, favor buttons always pertain to the theme of the convention.

# Chapter 1 Getting Started

Collectors judge the desirability of buttons based on many factors: subject matter or design; age; material; size; shape; and quality.

Quality has to do with the manufacture of the button. Was the button made exceptionally well or was the design particularly unique or gracious? Is it highly detailed or complex, unusually large or small, oddly shaped, or made of a rare material? Did the button stand out from the crowd because of an extra touch—a fancy border or an additional background material to set off the central design? Or perhaps the button should be considered special simply because it's particularly odd or funny or dramatic.

Although this one-piece copper button was die-stamped, the green and clear paste trim in the border was hand-set. The stamping added both an intricately detailed scene and an unusual three-dimensional shape and border to the button. The photo is enlarged to show the tiny deer standing to the left of center, barely visible when the button is seen at its normal 1″ size. Dating from the mid-twentieth century, this may have been a designer button.

The front of this silver-plated button is attractive, but the manufacturer's attention to detail can't be imagined until one looks at the back.

The same button from the back. It seems a shame to hide it, doesn't it? Notice the maker's mark E next to the shank.

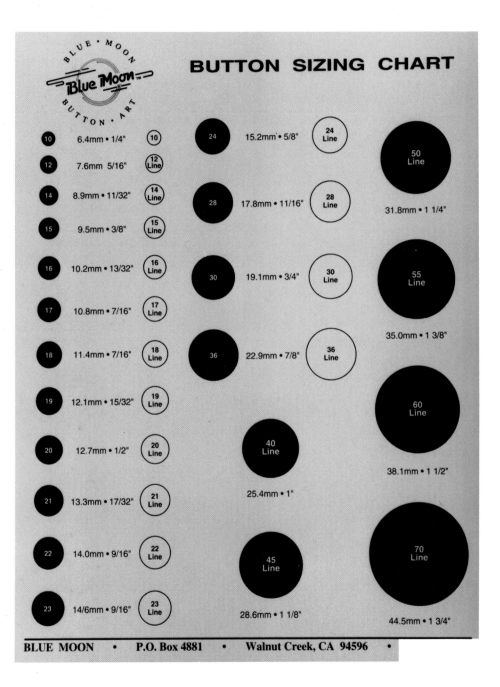

# BUTTON SIZING CHART

BLUE · MOON
Blue Moon™
BUTTON · ART

| | | | |
|---|---|---|---|
| **10** 6.4mm • 1/4" | **10** | **24** 15.2mm • 5/8" | **24 Line** |
| **12** 7.6mm 5/16" | **12 Line** | | **50 Line** |
| **14** 8.9mm • 11/32" | **14 Line** | **28** 17.8mm • 11/16" | **28 Line** |
| **15** 9.5mm • 3/8" | **15 Line** | | 31.8mm • 1 1/4" |
| **16** 10.2mm • 13/32" | **16 Line** | **30** 19.1mm • 3/4" | **30 Line** |
| **17** 10.8mm • 7/16" | **17 Line** | | **55 Line** |
| **18** 11.4mm • 7/16" | **18 Line** | **36** 22.9mm • 7/8" | **36 Line** |
| **19** 12.1mm • 15/32" | **19 Line** | | 35.0mm • 1 3/8" |
| **20** 12.7mm • 1/2" | **20 Line** | **40 Line** | **60 Line** |
| **21** 13.3mm • 17/32" | **21 Line** | 25.4mm • 1" | 38.1mm • 1 1/2" |
| **22** 14.0mm • 9/16" | **22 Line** | **45 Line** | **70 Line** |
| **23** 14/6mm • 9/16" | **23 Line** | 28.6mm • 1 1/8" | 44.5mm • 1 3/4" |

**BLUE MOON** • **P.O. Box 4881** • **Walnut Creek, CA 94596** •

Since the mid-nineteenth century, button manufacturers worldwide have used a French system known as *lignes* (lines) to describe button sizes. A manufacturer's ligne chart is shown here.

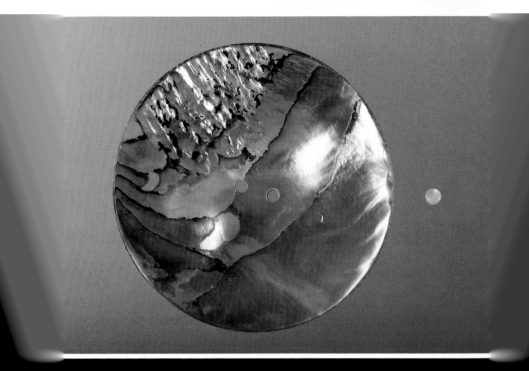

Mother-of-pearl buttons, sized from one extreme to the other.

ineteenth-century metal buttons were often manufactured in the three sizes shown. These
ictorian examples picture Cupid play-acting as Hyman, the God of Love, forging weddin

A button manufacturer's sample card of plastic buttons, 1960s.

Button collectors sort and display buttons based on several factors, including size. Competitors and judges use official measures to verify sizes; designations include large (over 1 ½"), medium (¾"-1 ½"), small (⅜"-¾"), and diminutive (under ⅜"). Sometimes, but not always, the size affects value: for instance, the Victorian metal picture buttons are far less expensive in the small sizes.

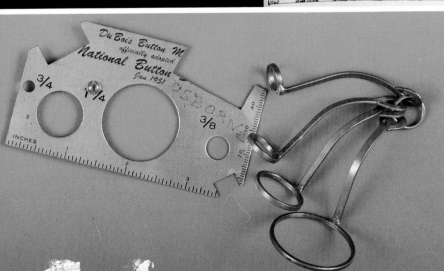

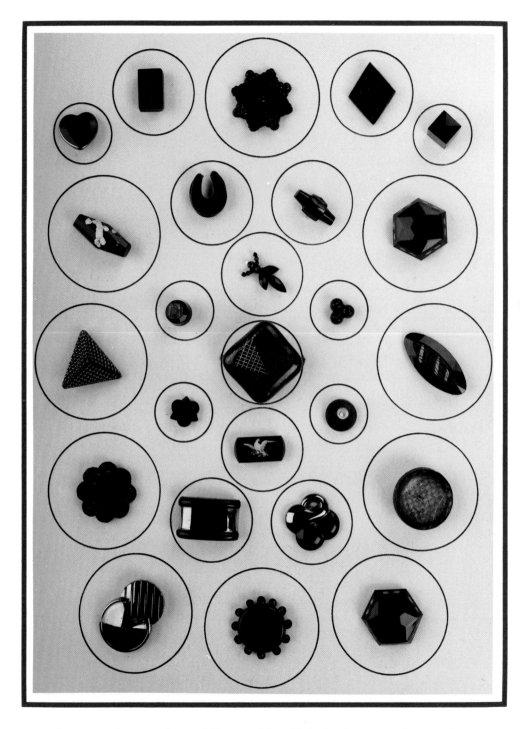

Buttons aren't necessarily round. No two of these black glass buttons are the same shape.

The many shapes of mother-of-pearl buttons.

Square buttons are a specialty of many collectors. Squares particularly abound in mother-of-pearl and black glass, though in competition, advanced collectors would have squares made of such materials as Wedgwood pottery, Satsuma pottery, ivory, silver, and so on. Seen in this grouping of "pearls" are cowrie shell at the far right, green snail, shaded pearl, trochus shell, and a pin-shanked abalone button.

Who wouldn't fall for buttons as funny as these? Yes, they really were originally made as clothing buttons. They are part of a huge category known as realistics—buttons that have the actual shape of the item portrayed. Realistics have been manufactured since the eighteenth century, though such examples are very rare. Those pictured here are twentieth-century examples made of metal, wood, Bakelite, plastic, glass, sterling, and enamel.

Wooden realistics, ca. 1930-1980.

Button collectors have given rise to a mini-industry: studio buttons made expressly for collectors. Because of the large number of collectors and artists involved, buttons have been made in a tremendous number of materials, techniques, and subjects. Most of them are very well designed and constructed. Some collectors ignore these non-commercial buttons entirely, but others seek them avidly. Any button sold to the general public, regardless of how "arty" or unusual, is not a studio button.

All of these studio buttons are the work of one Illinois craftsman, Janice Young. Multi-talented, she works in several mediums. Buttons pictured are of painted and carved wood, embossed and dyed leather, and fabric.

In the late 1970s, Debbie Reiter Skarda, a talented scrimshaw artist, made beautifully detailed studio buttons. She used antique mother-of-pearl buttons as the base for her etched designs. Her buttons are among the prettiest of all studio examples.

# Chapter 2  Button Construction:
## Fronts and Backs

These are two of the most common picture buttons from the Victorian era, the Trumpeter of Sackingen (Germany), and at right, the Sentinel of Cracow (Poland). They both commemorate historic events (which you can look up!.). Many beginning collectors buy them from an antiques dealer, and pay way too much for them!

During the late-nineteenth century, manufacturers offered a variety of dyed brass buttons in finishes to match the deep, muted shades of the era's fabrics. Reds and purples were the most usual; blue and green finishes are seldom seen. It's not always easy to find examples in the original tints: many collectors have inadvertently removed the coloring with metal polish.

Manufacturers often copied from one another, and popular subjects were reproduced as buttons in other materials. The button on the left is black glass; the right, brass. Both represent the Greek goddess Astraea, in her incarnation as a star. There was an absolute passion for mythological subjects from the late eighteenth to the mid-nineteenth centuries, in Germany, France, and England, the main centers of manufacture for metal picture buttons.

The child-like god of the south wind is shown in brass on the left, and carved in mother-of-pearl on the right.

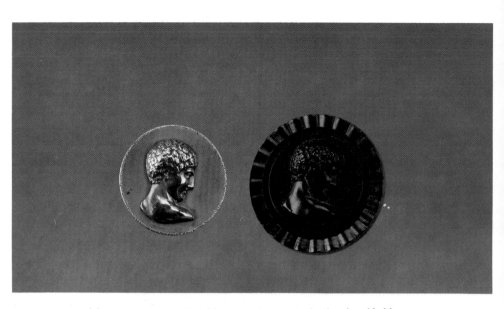

Mercury appears in tinted brass, and again, in dyed and molded horn.

Known as Roland and his Horn, the left button is made of tinted red brass. On the right is a different interpretation in brass by another manufacturer. Roland was the subject of an epic poem, popular with the mid-nineteenth-century public who had developed a fascination with medieval legends and heros.

---

By understanding the changes in button construction and materials used over the centuries, one can better judge the age of buttons. Also, because buttons reflect the culture and arts of their time, their surface designs may offer good clues as well. This dating method isn't infallible since many art styles are revived decades later, so a button's construction must be considered to determine its time of manufacture.

The apex of Victorian design, captured in a two-piece brass picture button.

These buttons aren't hard to date—they're called Gay Nineties. Very showy and ornate, the jewelled centers are glass; collectors seek a variety of colors and shapes in the "jewels."

A truly stunning mother-of-pearl button with a typically elegant Edwardian-era design; the base is engraved with leaves and lightly gilded. The iridescent-blue top layer, carved in relief in a palette shape, features an engraved bird entwined with a curving floral spray.

A very large, deluxe celluloid button from the early Art Nouveau era. The brass lady with her typically flowing hair rests on a thin wafer of off-white celluloid known as ivoroid, made to imitate the color and grained pattern of real ivory.

These Art Deco era buttons are made of celluloid, leather, lithographed wood, Bakelite, brass, and chrome.

Manufacturers often added borders and/or contrasting background materials to make buttons more exciting to the era's consumers. Many collectors specifically search out such examples.

Cupid was the subject of many, many buttons; this heavy one-piece brass example is one of the most desirable. Its fine workmanship (note the hand-engraving and chasing) and striking neo-classical design are complemented by the handkerchief-corner border. Made in the first half of the nineteenth century, handkerchief-corner buttons of any subject are eagerly sought by collectors, who pay a premium price for them; all are beautifully crafted and none are common.

Cupid is holding on to horns of plenty in this two-piece tinted brass picture button from the late nineteenth century. It is set off by a dotted cut-through border, sparkling because there is a mirror-finished layer of tin sandwiched between the front and back of the button. There are many metal buttons with sparkly backgrounds; the majority are modern and known as "Twinkles."

The Fire Fairy is a late Victorian brass picture button with a heart and *fleur-de-lis* border. Judging from the numerous buttons of different designs that are found with this border, it must have been very popular; there are collectors who even specialize in heart-bordered buttons. This odd fairy—rendered in such detail that even her navel shows—is among the more unusual ones.

Both this and the following picture feature buttons of Hector, the ancient Trojan hero, but the manufacturers took great pains to make theirs the more exciting. Both have been given special borders, to the delight of today's collectors. This one features stalking panthers, one of the nicest of the many border designs found on Victorian-era buttons.

This Hector has a double border, the outer one diaper-cut and the inner one a curlicue design. The button itself has an unusual construction: the entire center was cut-out and the central figure (as well as the sewing shank on the reverse) is attached to a bar riveted across the back of the button.

The linked chain border is the dominant feature of this button; it's so three-dimensional that it looks added, but isn't. The dyed brass is engraved and has a mother-of-pearl disc at its center. It dates from the turn of the twentieth century.

A deluxe under-glass button from France (c. 1790-1810) with an Oriental scene painted on parchment, set in brass, and rimmed with a paste border.

A wonderfully balanced design made in pierced brass, perfectly set-off by a geometric leaf border. The Victorians seem to have loved buttons with children on them: many designs feature them.

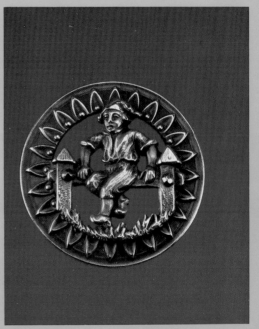

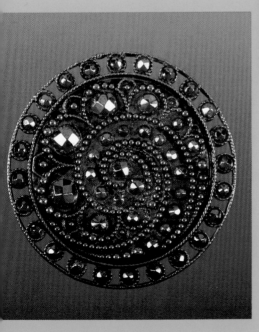

This lovely, large brass button of conventional (non-pictorial) design has a spiral pattern enhanced with faceted cut-steels riveted on in descending size and features a pierced, cut-steel border. Ca.1880.

Can you imagine this button without the pearl background? The basic design is fabulous, but with the pearl, it's perfection. This gilded brass snake from the Art Nouveau era both borders the button and acts as its central theme, an unusual combination. Button makers employed contrasting backgrounds for a strong visual effect, and in this case succeeded marvelously.

The pearl background on this button is abalone shell, chosen for its drama and color. The high-sided, drum-shaped brass button dates from the British Arts and Crafts period, pre-dating the previous example by three or more decades.

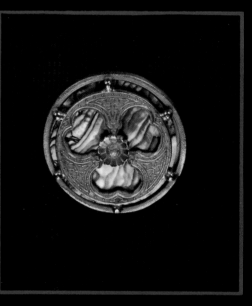

One of a number of opera-theme buttons, this pressed steel has a delightful floral border and a separate pearl background. The darkly iridescent pearl was chosen for its moody evening sky appearance, the nacre (shimmer) giving the impression of moonlight. Contemporary with the debut of Herbert's opera, *The Red Mill*, and named for it, this deluxe button features a brass windmill with a fancy-cut steel sail riveted to it.

A mythological creature, a pretty border, and a screen background decorate a Victorian brass button. Screen backgrounds aren't particularly easy to find.

This eighteenth-century, copper-rimmed button features an open-worked steel star with a milk-glass background. It has an iron back, typical of buttons of this era.

This is High-Victorian design at its best, showing with a winged cherub riding in a fanciful chariot, grasping a grotesque mask in one hand and a fern in the other. The tinted tin button has a celluloid sheet background. A new invention for manufacturers to toy with, such backgrounds represent the first use of celluloid in buttons, ca. 1880.

**25**

A brass Neptune rises from the sea in front of a wooden background. The button's construction and the baroque sculptural-style design date it to the mid-Victorian period.

The velvet backgrounds of these brass buttons epitomize the soft elegance of ladies during the late Victorian era. Very small velvet-backs were used as perfume buttons, but these larger examples were strictly decorative.

It's very often the design on the front of buttons that appeals to collectors but for purposes of identification, the backs hold at least as much, if not more, importance.

The reverse of a sterling-silver button showing the hallmarks and maker's initials. Collectors love sterling buttons for their quality and beauty; they are also a cinch to identify and date. Books can be consulted to interpret the markings on silver items from all over the world. The mark seen here proves the origin of this button to be London, 1907.

On the right is the most popular button backmark, T. W. and W., Paris (Trelon, Weil and Weil company) from France. Some collectors have large specialized collections of "Paris backs," as these are known (the backmarks must include the word "Paris"). Although the T.W. and W. mark is perhaps the most desired, marks from other companies are also sought, such as that shown on the left, AP and Cie. Breveté, Paris. (*Breveté* means patented.) This was Albert Parent and Company of Paris, the manufacturer of some of the most elegant buttons ever made.

A German manufacturing mark found on many brass picture buttons is *Eingetragen* (registered). Many buttons (including a large percentage of the nineteenth-century metal picture buttons) are of German origin.

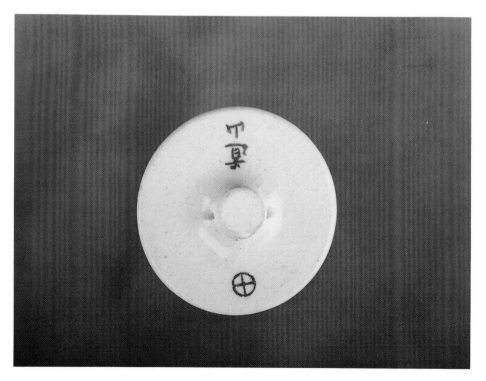

Backmarks on Japanese Satsuma pottery are actually quite unreliable. Many marks were copied over the years and most Satsuma buttons carry no marks. Aside from the novelty, they add no status or value to the button.

Molded horn buttons were sometimes backmarked, most often with *Caen* (a town in France.) An old-fashioned term for a horn button is "pick-back", which referred to the little hole often left in the back of the button after it was removed, with the aid of a sharp pick, from the mold.

Button backs are also important for their shanks: the different attachment methods and materials used often give the single best clue to the button's age. The most basic form of attachment is simply a thread through a hole. Buttons with sewing holes are known as **sew-throughs**. The usual number of holes is two or four, but there are buttons with one, three, and five holes.

One holed-buttons are called **whistles**; they really have two holes on the back, but only one shows from the top. Few modern whistle buttons have been made. There are also examples of one-holed buttons that really do have only the one hole; usually eighteenth-century or earlier, this is seen in Wedgwood, old Chinese jades, and so on. The thread was brought up through the hole, drawn through a tiny, separate gold or pearl bead (which then sat atop the button) and back down through the same button-hole.

**Thread-back shanks** were used on a limited number of early to mid-nineteenth century buttons. Threadbacks have a radiating web of thread wound tightly around the button back, held in place by an added rim. The attaching thread was run underneath this web. These are fragile buttons and the threads have often broken.

Many buttons, old and new, have **self-shanks**. Self-shanks are those which are made from the same material as the button body, and are either carved or molded with it. Glass, wood, ivory, jade, vegetable ivory, plastics, and other buttons have commonly been made with self-shanks.

Some buttons had metal shanks which went right through the body of the button; known as **pin-shanks**, they can be distinguished by the small knob of metal atop the button. Pin-shanks were commonly used in the eighteenth-century, often on pearl, bone, ivory, and wooden buttons. They were not in widespread use later than the early-nineteenth century.

Other **attached** shanks include those that are glued on, such as may be seen on many celluloid buttons, and metal ones that are inserted into semi-molten metal, glass, or molded horn button-bodies. These are either metal **loop-shanks** (usually brass) or brass **box-shanks** (shaped like a cube with a hole tunneled through). There are, additionally, many metal buttons with loop shanks that were braised or soldered on.

Pad shanks are commonly found on fabric buttons. The fabric pad protrudes through a hole in the metal button back; the thread was sewn through the pad.

Thread-back buttons.

All four of these sew-throughs are made of china.

Modern glass buttons (post 1918) with molded self-shanks.

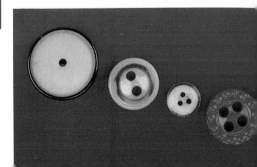

Antique whistle buttons: from top right, china; black glass with inlaid pearl center; the back of a whistle button showing the two holes on the reverse; a glass watch-crystal button; dyed and engraved brass; and at center, an inlaid composition (mixed materials molded together) button.

Attached celluloid shanks on celluloid buttons.

Antique metal buttons with various types of added brass shanks, pre-1918. Top, Paris back with birdcage shank; left, soldered loop shank on one piece pressed metal button; right top, inserted loop shank, bottom left, an unusual triple bar shank; bottom right, a bar shank.

A ribbon-like bar shank stretches across the back of this button and attaches at both ends. The sewing loop is braised onto the bar.

Possibly the most unique button shanks ever devised are the patented face shanks of Battersea Ltd.'s pewter buttons manufactured in the late 1970s. This face is a very faithful portrait of the firm's founder and president; two other faces were used as well. The face shanks were used only on solid pewter buttons—the firm's plated buttons were molded with plain shanks. All were back-marked with the company's name and the date of manufacture. Since 1980 Battersea has made no buttons for the general public, but has instead concentrated on custom-designed buttons for private and corporate clients.

Glass button backs from the mid-nineteenth century include several clues to their age. **Swirl-backs** have rings of concentric circles in the glass around the inserted brass loopshanks. **Scissors-backs** have a raised line bisecting the button-back, caused by a bit of excess glass oozing out when the mold was closed. **Screen-backs** occurred when the still-hot glass buttons were laid above a screen to cool, thus transferring the pattern to the glass. Although swirl-backs are seen (rarely) on modern glass, scissors-backs and screen-backs appear only on antique glass buttons.

Various backs and shanks found on antique glass buttons: top right, a screen-back; middle right, a molded self-shank; center top and middle, embedded brass shanks with shank-plates; bottom center and left, inserted brass shanks with shank-plates; top left and center, swirl-backs.

Black glass button backs include, at left, an embedded brass box-shank; bottom left and right, embedded shank plates, one in a rosette shape; center, a molded self-shank; top right, a swirlback; far right, a metal back-plate with a soldered shank. These are all antique examples.

Sometimes buttons are worthy of saving, yet have no real value. These buttons from high-button shoes, for example, are of no monetary consequence, yet who would want to thr~~ow~~ out such relics from the past? This fun mounting is a perfect compromise.

This huge pair (shown actual size, pictured sideways so they will fit on the page!) of silver filigree buttons were made for a Dutchman to wear at the waist of his baggy pants. There is a maker's mark stamped on the front edge of one of them. Extremely rare, these probably date from the 1600s.

Cape and cloak buttons from the past are among the most dramatic and elegant ever made. This humorous carved and pierced art-nouveau style example is the largest mother-of-pearl button (3½" in diameter) I have ever seen. It still has its original French label on the reverse. The enameled center is set in a metal frame and rivited to the back. Made to be worn at the top of a lady's formal cape, it has two metal shanks on the back to help distribute its weight on the fabric.

**Opposite page:**

These unusual ladies' coat buttons from the 1930s were evidently not manufactured at any other time. Each consists of a decorative front chained to a separate circular brass disc; holes in the disc enabled it to be sewn onto the coat. The reverse side of the top piece has a protruding bump which snaps onto the disc, through the buttonhole, to close the coat. When not "buttoned," the front just dangles on the chain. The vast majority of these fasteners were humorous; materials include brass, pewter-like metals, wood, Sirocco (molded wood pulp), celluloid, and glass.

Blazers and sportscoats have melded in many people's minds, but they had very different origins. Hunting jackets were worn on country hunts and shooting expeditions for more than two centuries and had finely crafted buttons featuring animals, birds, scenes of hunters, fishermen, and so on. Members of private clubs (usually fox hunts) wore jackets with custom-made buttons, often with the club's initials or logo.

Sporting buttons from the nineteenth century, of gilded brass and sterling silver; those with people or exotic animals pictured are the most desirable.

Eighteenth-century hunt club buttons of engraved silver. The oval example with the engraved fox is brass.

The blazer jacket originated with English boating club members late in the nineteenth century. There had been special lounging and smoking coats worn in men's clubs, hunting coats for sporting events, and so on, but these were still serious clothes of fine materials. When young men took to wearing brightly striped, lightweight white jackets on their excursions, the colorful, informal appearance was at first ridiculed with the pejorative descriptive phrase "blazing bright." Tremendous numbers of blazer buttons have been made in the years since, of every type and quality. Modern retail blazers usually have had unimpressive buttons. Special-order blazer button sets have been made for more discerning customers; these are often exceptional.

The brass buttons at the top are top-quality blazer monogram buttons made in England, ca. 1900. The remainder, all modern, are enamelled, leather, pewter, silver, and inexpensive metal. Sporting buttons from the nineteenth century of gilded brass and sterling silver; those with people or exotic animals represented are most desirable.

Highly-detailed modern blazer buttons by the Ben Silver company of Charleston, South Carolina. Corporate clients order custom buttons, as do political organizations (including the White House), private schools and universities, and so on. Pictured are various custom-made buttons in brass, gilt, and enamelled metal. *Courtesy Robert Prenner.*

Nineteenth-century waistcoat (men's vest) buttons were made in great variety. Often glass-centered, small brass buttons, they usually had long loop shanks. The button at the bottom of the photo is a door-knocker complete with a moveable ivory ring.

Uniform buttons of all types are collected, and the military buttons in particular are avidly sought by specialists: whole books are dedicated to this subject. Other specialties include airline, railroad, and steamship lines, firemen, corporate uniform, and so on. The most specialized collection I have ever seen was made up of nothing but staff buttons from different British insane asylums. That was dedication! Many button collectors ignore uniform buttons altogether, not wishing to involve themselves in the study.

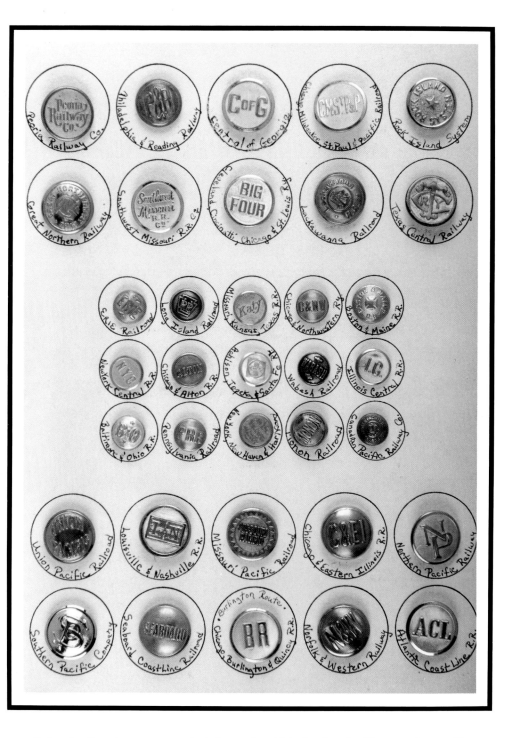

Railroad uniform buttons are particularly popular with both railroad and button collectors. The mounted card of buttons shown contains examples from 35 different railroads. Collectors are most interested in those from defunct rail lines.

Gloves were once an important part of life for the properly dressed woman. Buttoned tightly to wrists and arms, gloves had from one to sixteen buttons. The unique shank—a flattened metal shank in a U-shape, attached to the rim of a large hole in the button-back—determines whether a small button was used on a glove or elsewhere. (Enlarged in photo.)

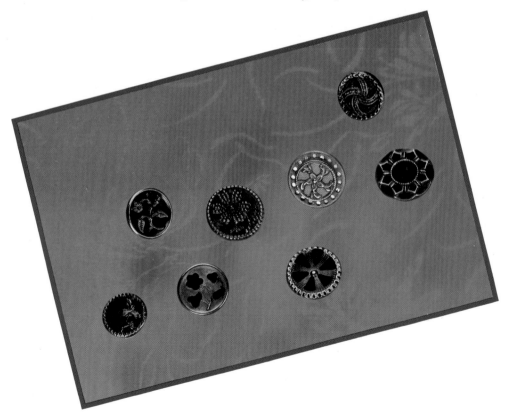

Small brass buttons with velvet backgrounds were sometimes used for perfume: When saturated with a favorite scent by the wearer, the absorbent velvet gave off the fragrance for a long while.

Another type of perfume button was sold during the 1940s: the molded plastic cameo unscrewed and the cup-like bottom held a cake of solid perfume or rouge. A few of the examples in collections are still filled. The rouge buttons have no marks on the back, but the ones that held perfume do: this one says jasmine. The fronts are identical except for color variations. Even more surprising than the secret compartment itself is the maker of these ultra-feminine little cuties: the Colt Firearms Manufacturing Company!

This small ivory baseball button also unscrews; it definitely held something at one time, for it's been carefully hollowed out inside. I know of a similar button which held two little ivory dice. Ca. 1910.

Two views of one of the most sought-after military buttons of the World War II era, the United States General Service locket button. Unless you know the backmark—Liberty Mfg. Co., Los Angeles, Cal.—there is no way to differentiate these from the vast numbers of other buttons that look exactly the same but do not open. It is easy to find the side clasp, but if you don't know to look for it, you'd never notice it. Similar American and British air force uniform buttons with hidden compass interiors were worn by pilots in case they were shot down and needed to find their way on the ground in a strange land. (The English version unscrews rather than lifts open.)

Here's a brand-new type of novelty button! I don't know of any other jigsaw-puzzle buttons. This adorable set—a boy and girl, each made up of four interlocking plastic pieces—is a 1992 import. *Courtesy of Blue Moon*

Buttons were often sold in sets: the buttons may be alike, or they may be designed or shaped differently yet related in some way.

Still in the original case with the fastening clips, this is a set of six pearl waistcoat buttons mounted in brass. They have simulated thread, made of gold wire, and pretend holes, with large brass loop shanks in the backs.

Now scarce, various button sets featuring cigarette packs were manufactured in the 1930s and 1940s. Very realistic, the small buttons have faithful copies of labels from the actual brands of that time. Some were plastic, others (which look like brass) are actually gold-colored celluloid with paper labels attached. Do not clean these—you'll ruin them!

In the 1930s, a mania began for realistically-shaped, small plastic, celluloid, or glass buttons. The fad was gone by the early 1950s, but for two decades, countless sets of these buttons, known as Goofies, were manufactured. At left, the Circus set was very popular; so many were manufactured they are not hard to find today. In contrast, the 1930s Child's Toys set—a doll, carriage, teddy bear, clown, and drum—is rather hard to find.

There is a trend right now for buttons to be made into jewelry. Button collectors hate it; the rest of the world seems to love it. The real question is whether or not the integrity of the button is destroyed. It's a shame to break (by removing the shank) a button—a form of jewelry itself—in order to glue it on to another piece of jewelry. However, when the button can be converted without destroying it, perhaps there is nothing wrong in it.

I recently saw an artist at a fair with brooches made from buttons. The shanks had been yanked off, glue had been glopped all over them, and the buttons were piled up. One brooch was made from a large Bakelite base with several smaller celluloid and glass buttons glued atop, and finally, in a travesty of everything an artist should have held dear, the back of an eighteenth-century button—an under-glass painting on ivory was broken off and it was glued to the others. Once a miniature work of fine art, a two-hundred-year-old French button was now merely part of an ugly collage.

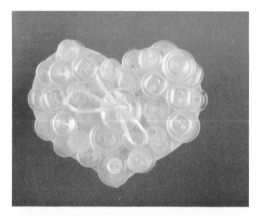

Ubiquitous plastic shirt buttons glued to a wooden brooch.

A button bracelet with fun buttons and a beautiful design. Crocheted button bracelets are a non-destructive use of buttons. Today, artists are designing and selling button jewelry, often with special themes such as bracelets of scotty dog buttons, or fruit-shaped buttons, or nautical-themed red, white, and blue buttons. *Courtesy of artist Judy Snow, Bygone Buttonwear.*

The conversion of totally run-of-the-mill buttons into craft supplies is harmless; the use of collectible or historic buttons as jewelry is also fine, when used in a temporary, non-destructive way. Glorious old buttons can be worn hanging on a chain, or as a brooch, pinned on with a safety pin through the shank.

These three valuable buttons have been turned into jewelry: an extremely rare, extra large Japanese Arita porcelain head; a gorgeous, large, Chinese white jade flower, ca. 1700; and a red-tinted, Victorian-era brass.

The brass picture-button still has its shank on back, but a wire loop has been soldered to the top to accommodate a neck chain. This $5.00 necklace would have been a $25.00 button to a collector. The Arita head has a pin firmly clamped onto the two molded self-shanks on the back. Although the shanks remain, they probably would break if the pin were removed. This was purchased as a pin for $40.00. As an Arita button, its value would be closer to $150.00 for its rare size and shape.

The jade flower—a first rate example of the type of dimensional carving prevalent at the beginning of the Chien-L'ung period—was originally a sew-through button (you can see the two sewing holes in the center) which was carefully converted to a dress clip around 1915, judging from the sterling mounting which was custom-crafted and has a Chinese silversmith's mark. The mounting cradles the button by curving lightly around the petals and can easily and safely be removed. $10.00 was paid for the clip at a flea market while in button circles it would have been worth well over $100.00. Dealers might do better to find a button collector than to convert buttons into jewelry!

# Chapter 4  Foolers and Look-alikes

Buttons have been made in almost every material. By recognizing a button's material, one can better judge its age. Some materials were used to make buttons for only a relatively short time. It is by no means always easy to identify the material from which a button was made. To make matters really difficult, manufacturers often purposely made look-alikes to resemble other materials that were either too costly, too rare, or too difficult with which to work.

Okay, lets identify this stunning rococo foliate design. Sterling silver? No, its ivory.

The reverse shows the shanked ivory button. Capped with pierced sterling, this elegant button was probably from the French fin-du-siécle period.

Three black cameos in oval-shaped buttons that seem to be quite similar, but are not at all. At left is a dyed and molded horn button, ca. 1850; in the center is a pressed, hollow celluloid button, ca. 1930; and the right button is made of molded black glass set in a brass mounting, ca. 1880.

This would appear to be a metal button with a lovebird design.
The reverse of the lovebirds shows it to be a nylon button! Made in Paris during the 1970 to 1990 period, this is a so-called "faced button" with an aluminum shell clamped over the nylon back.

These are all celluloid buttons in imitation of various other materials: wood, leather, ribbon, silver, faceted black glass, pierced bone, baise-taille enamelwork, carved coral, moiré fabric, vegetable ivory, mother-of-pearl, tortoise shell, and amber. They range in date from the 1890s to the late 1940s.

A grouping of black glass buttons, all of which were designed and colored to resemble popular fabrics of the Victorian and Edwardian eras.

Imitation tortoise shell buttons made from plastics, celluloid, Bakelite, and glass, dating from the 1940s when this look was in vogue. Real tortoise shell buttons are not common.

A group of modern plastic buttons, dating from about 1940 to 1990, imitating brass, silver, pewter, copper, inlaid glass, pressed wood, leather, glass paperweights, agate, gemstones, vegetable ivory, pearlized glass, mirrored glass, ceramic, china calicoes, natural horn, and mother-of-pearl.

# Chapter 5  Buttons from Everywhere

Every country in the world has had a button industry of one sort or another. Buttons have always been among the items sold, traded, or carried between lands, and this practice continues today. Collectors have a world of wonders from which to choose.

Dating from 1940 to 1980, these are buttons from around the world. At top left is a papiér-mâché mask button from Sri Lanka. The sterling silver fan came from Japan, and the carved pearl set in sterling, from Israel. The black onyx and silver button is Mexican and the two ivory buttons on the right came from Alaska and Canada.

Mexico has been the source of many wonderful buttons. This twentieth-century assortment features, from the top, three copper masks, a terrific silver face with a ring through the nose, and Aztec-inspired images in copper on brass, jade set in silver, and beaten silver.

This large, sterling llama was made in Peru almost fifty years ago, circa 1945, but in button-collecting parlance, that's modern.

Sterling silver buttons with masks and religious images from Ecuador, ca. 1930s and 1940s.

Old Chinese buttons are a real challenge to date! These three bugs all are well beyond the century mark. The butterfly was made with cloisonné enamel, the moth is a sterling toggle-type, and the cicada has transparent enamel over copper and silver.

Siam was the source of this huge, répoussé silver button decorated with a sword dancer. The age is difficult to determine, but from its heavy weight and fine workmanship, it probably pre-dates 1800.

Persian miniature paintings on camel bone, and a painted Persian enamel set in silver. Many were exported from Iran by button dealers in the 1940s, but by then some were already found in button collections. It is safe to date them before the middle of the twentieth century.

From pre-W.W.II Japan came this set of realistically-shaped ivory brush and comb buttons, with Shibayama-style mother-of-pearl and coral inlay work.

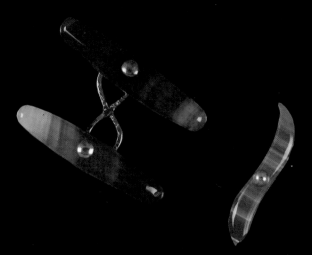

**Agate** buttons with gold pinshanks from the nineteenth century. The pair at the left have been looped together to form a toggle.

**Alligator** skin was rarely used for buttons, but this one was worth the wait! Oversized and very thick, it's a hand-stitched designer button from the 1930s. The brass alligator sewn on the front is a playful touch.

**Amethyst,** a semi-precious stone, used to be rather rare and quite a bit more expensive that it is now that more sources have been discovered. It was seldom used for buttons: this Victorian-era set would have been quite special. *Sandra Dieckmann collection.*

**Antlers** were carved into wonderful buttons during the nineteenth century, most commonly in the Black Forest area of Germany where they were quite popular as Victorian travel souvenirs (three are pictured at center). Plain staghorn and antler buttons are sold today (upper left and lower right) for casual wear, but collectors are interested only in the carved examples.

**Bamboo** hasn't often been used for buttons. These twentieth-century examples include a plastic-trimmed deerfoot shape.

---

**Bakelite**, the first all-synthetic plastic, was invented in 1909 but not really used for jewelry or buttons until the late twenties when it suddenly became—along with celluloid—the material of choice for large, creative, colorful buttons. The thirties and forties belonged to Bakelite and celluloid, but by 1950, they were both displaced by newer and cheaper plastics. Bakelite buttons are not at all easy to find: button collectors (who ignored them totally until quite recently) have been spurred into action by the many Bakelite jewelry aficionados who have been snapping up buttons as fast as they can. Prices have skyrocketed.

Desirable types of **Bakelite** buttons include these striking opaque and transparent combinations, the scarce marbled version in the bottom right, and the rare, tri-colored, inlaid type at center.

Reverse carving on transparent Bakelite, one of its most attractive incarnations. Here the carved-out area was carefully painted making the flowers look as though they're enclosed. Unlike Lucite, clear Bakelite has yellowed with time.

Bakelite at its whimsical best: a silver-plated hand on a Bakelite base, a rare realistic clown, and a little suitcase dangling through a ring on the front of a sew-through button.

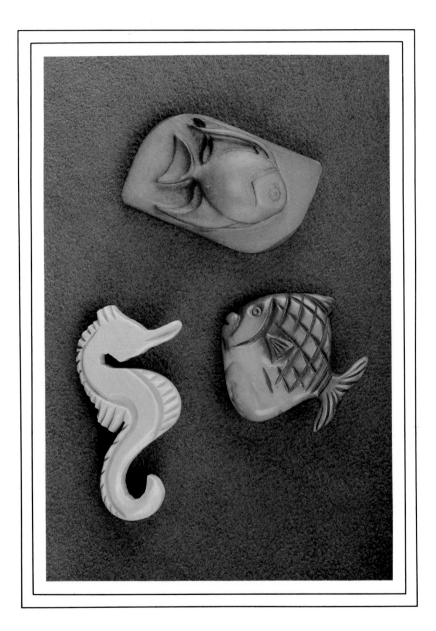

Bakelite buttons were never better than when carved and shaped like these deluxe, unusual examples. The top fish is hand-carved in relief and the fat fish is beautifully colored and engraved. The seahorse is simply perfect in its simplicity.

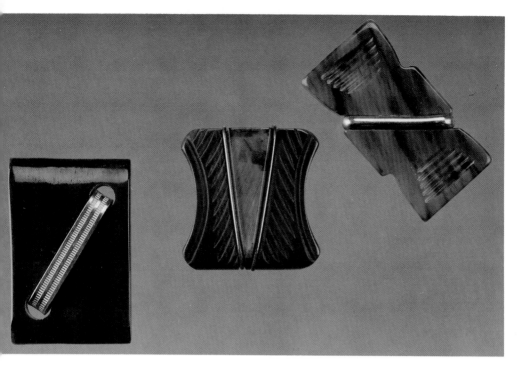

Ladies coat buttons of Bakelite, trimmed with brass, demonstrate their design origin in the Art Deco era.

Cookies! Button collectors have suddenly gone crazy for these. Made during the thirties, in celluloid as well as Bakelite, they were named after the sliced roll cookies they resemble; cookie buttons always have the same design, front and back, but are not necessarily flat and round. The striking colors and geometric Deco lines certainly add to their appeal.

Black glass buttons were made by the millions from about 1840 until about 1965. Thousands of different examples can be found. England's Queen Victoria went through such a long period of mourning that she popularized black fashions and stimulated the black glass industry. Although her buttons and jewelry were of jet, this mineral was not mined in enough quantity to satisfy the vast public demand so black glass became the primary substitute. Once the black button industry was in full production, the creative and varied designs kept black glass stylish for decades.

Iridescent black glass buttons date from the nineteenth century, pre-dating carnival glass by several decades: Iridescent examples with pictures molded on them are most popular with button collectors. Most are small.

Silver-lustred black glass buttons are found in large sizes like these nineteenth century examples, but far fewer have pictorial designs than do iridescent ones. There are also many twentieth-century silvered black glass buttons.

Riveted **black glass** buttons, made in the late-nineteenth-century, are remarkably complex. Each bead of glass is attached to a tiny metal pin and riveted through the metal base. Dramatic yet fragile in appearance, they are too labor intensive to have been attempted in modern times.

Brass, steel, and mother-of-pearl inlays were used to trim black glass buttons during the last century. There are no similar modern ones.

During the nineteenth century, button manufacturers often mounted glass in metal frames. The molded-glass cameo head at the left is a "Victorian jewel," a medium-sized metal button with a molded or decorated glass center. The "small jewels" at the bottom include an early Italian micro-mosaic of excellent quality and an unusual example with a paperweight-style center. (Button enlarged by ½.)

These black glass buttons from the mid-Victorian age are hand painted using many different techniques. They are not particularly expensive and are quite attractive.

This specialized type of painted black-glass button is reminiscent of Mary Gregory glass and contemporary to it. The paintings are sometimes done with great skill.

Lacy-patterned black, clear, and camphor glass is always striking, especially when mounted in metal, as seen here. Although these black and opaque lacies (ca.1850-1915) are gorgeous, the clear glass unmounted examples are preferred, and so these are far less expensive.

Dating black glass buttons is tricky. Old black glass lustre buttons have metal loop shanks or molded self shanks; modern ones hardly ever have metal shanks. Old glass usually has scratches and crazing on the back, and sometimes a patent date (1881), but no company name. Only on modern (post-1918) buttons are backmarks such as B.G.E. (Bailey, Green and Elger, Inc.), or Le Chic or La Mode (B. Blumenthal and Company, Inc. tradenames; La Mode is the fine line, and Le Chic, from 1932 to now, is the less expensive line).

These West German, iridescent black glass buttons were made in the 1950s and 1960s. They are often somewhat larger than the ones of a century earlier, and definitely more garish.

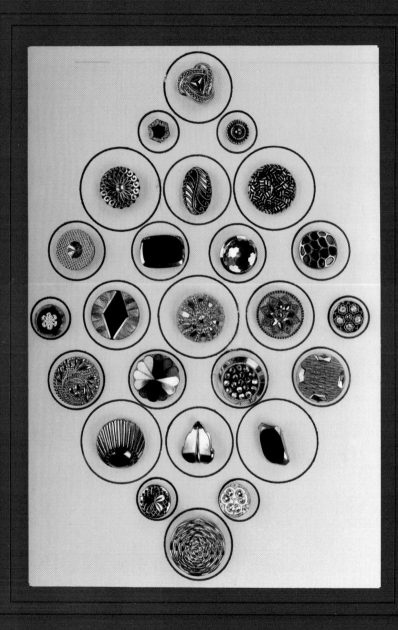

Modern West German and Czechoslovakian black glass buttons with gold lustre. When some of the black shows through the lustre, the button is referred to as "parti-lustred."

Bone, mostly from cattle, has been turned into buttons for at least three centuries. The most mundane of the nineteenth-century's buttons were little bone underwear buttons, many of which are still in Grandma's old button box. Pin-shanked larger discs of bone were popular in the eighteenth century and ranged from starkly simple to rather attractive. The upper left button, with its steel pinshank and decorative edging, is attractive. The center dyed example is a la Victorian lady's button with an aesthetic dragonfly/floral design. The top center button has a complex transfer printed design, a technique usually found on ceramics. The remaining buttons were all worn by men and date from the early nineteenth century.

**Celluloid**, invented in 1870, was the first man-made plastic. Within a few years, it was being used as a background material for fine metal buttons. Solid celluloid buttons began to appear around 1890 and by the 1920s it was displacing vegetable ivory as the premier button material. Celluloid's ability to take dye and be shaped by molding, modeling, stamping, pulling, hollow-blowing, and machine-tooling techniques, made it enormously popular with manufacturers. Some of the most exciting buttons ever made were of celluloid; so were nearly all the most ugly. Unfortunately celluloid had a fatal flaw: it was extremely flammable. As soon as safer plastics were invented, celluloid was doomed. It was not used commercially after World War II except in Japan, and soon disappeared altogether.

**Celluloid** buttons can be found in a wide range of sizes, as demonstrated here by a small and a large example. The lady's head is an applied, silver-plated escutcheon.

**Opposite page:**
These Victorian celluloid buttons are mounted in metal or trimmed with metal. Large metal picture buttons were the rage during the last two decades of the nineteenth century, and these have the same "look." The average size is just over 1 ½" in diameter.

There's no mistaking one of these! They are "glow-bubbles" that date from the 1920s and consist of a metal base with a shiny foil or tin coating, covered with a hollow, semi-transparent bubble of celluloid. (Buttons in photo are reduced in size by half.)

These celluloid buttons are "ivoroids," made late in the nineteenth century. They are similar to stamped metal picture buttons, but the centers are die-stamped celluloid. They tend to be quite expensive. The bottom button is engraved sheet celluloid. The average size is just over 1½" in diameter. (Reduced in size by half.)

Nothing but fun! Celluloid buttons with naturalistic designs, and one wooden button trimmed with a red celluloid lobster.

**China** buttons for underwear, shirts, and dresses were manufactured from the 1840s on, in France, England, and on Long Island in the U.S. These were the average man's and woman's mainstay, going West on the wagon trains, being shipped to the gold fields of Alaska, the vineyards of France and the coal mines of England. Pioneers needed sturdy clothing and solid, practical buttons, and small chinas fit the bill. There are a number of different types, but the calicoes are the collectors' favorites.

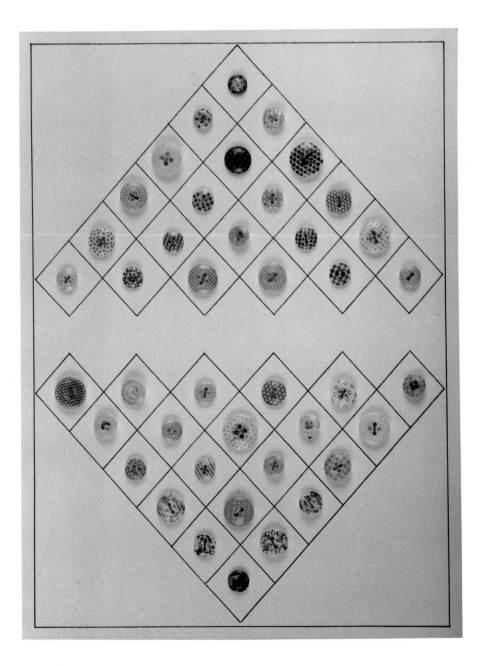

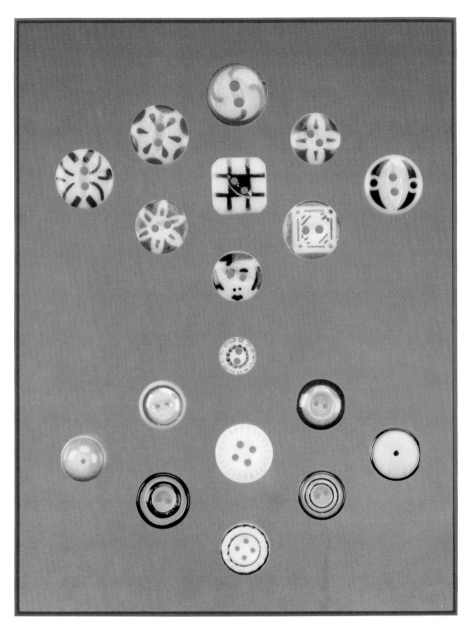

An assortment of small china buttons, the bottom group from the nineteenth century. The patterned buttons in the top group are called "stencils," after their method of decoration, and they are known to have been sold as late as the 1930s. When and where they were first made is a mystery; some claim their origin as Czechoslovakia. Nearly sixty stencil patterns are known.

**Opposite page:**
Decorated by transfer patterns which matched the calico fabrics of the period, these small china buttons are collected by pattern (over 325 designs have been cataloged so far) and color. Medium sized calicoes, and any that are rimmed with or set-in metal are particularly rare.

**Cinnabar** is a crimson-colored lacquer from China; when thickly layered onto a wooden or metal base, it can be beautifully carved. Buttons made of cinnabar date from the twentieth century; many were imported during the Oriental craze of the twenties. Floral designs are usual, but birds and people are also found. Oddities include lacquer carvings in colors other than red (black, green, white), large examples, and odd or realistic shapes.

**Coconut-shell** buttons have been made in realistic shapes—strictly for the tourist trade—in most tropical locations. Until the mid-1960s, when replaced by wood and plastic, Hawaiian-style shirts had plain sew-through coconut-shell buttons; this undoubtedly represents the largest commercial use of coconut shell for buttons.

**Coral** buttons are rare. The best were carved cameos, but all are hard to find. They were made in the nineteenth century in Italy. The carved knot button has an 18K gold shank; the button on the left has a pearl inlay and a self shank; the ball-shaped button has a sterling silver pin shank.

**Cork** buttons are certainly not plentiful—in fact they are rare, but not valuable. This large sized, modern button, ca. 1950, with a brass sailboat escutcheon, was probably used on an informal sports outfit.

**Damascene** is a type of decorative metalwork. Invented in Damascus centuries ago, it reached its finest development in the famous swords from Toledo, Spain. Old damascene buttons are quite rare. Many modern examples were made in Japan, as were those shown here. The work is done on a base of steel, gold, or brass, with gold and sterling inlays. A 24K mark appears on the upper left button.

**Diamonds** are certainly rare in buttons since so valuable a material was reused when fashions changed. This twentieth-century button (probably a hand-made designer creation from the 1920s) is black onyx with rhodonite and a diamond in the center. (Rhodonite is an unusual stone which was popular in Czarist Russia for jewelry and **objets-du-vertu**.) The reverse side is astounding: it's sharply cut with an all-over sunburst pattern and the wire shank is platinum.

**Enamels** comprise a large and popular category of buttons. Beginning with earlier Chinese and eighteenth-century French and English buttons, and continuing to the present, every type of enameling has been used on buttons. In many cases, more than one enameling technique is combined on a single button—for instance, one with a painted-enamel center may have a champlevé-enamel border. While the best enamels are among the most expensive buttons, there are others available for every budget. If you don't recognize the different enameling techniques, be cautious about from whom the buttons are purchased, and how much you pay.

Chinese **cloisonné** enamel buttons such as this date from the turn of the twentieth century. The word *cloisonné* comes from the French word for small cells, *cloisons*. (Cloistered monks, for example, live in cloisons.) To make a cloisonné enamel, small ribbons of metal are stood on edge and soldered to a metal base, making an outline of a pattern, like the walls of a maze. The resulting cells are filled with powdered glass of the desired colors and fired at a high temperature. The glass melts, resulting in a smooth, multi-colored enamel surface. Old cloisonné buttons are all considered rare: few are found.

This large pair of early Japanese cloisonné buttons is of extraordinary quality. They appear to be fine paintings rather than enamels, for the technique is so well mastered that one requires a magnifier to see the tiny ribbons of metal and individual cloisons.

**Basse-taille** enameling, also called guilloché, is simple to recognize: engine-turned designs were engraved on a metal base and covered with delicately colored, transparent enamel. This button, set in a late-nineteenth century hallmarked sterling frame, is French.

**Champlevé** enamels are imitations of cloisonné enamels and are far more common in buttons. Instead of the soldered metal walls, champlevé enamels have a die-stamped base with raised outlines and recessed spaces which are filled with powdered glass and fired. Champlevé enamels are far less labor-intensive and subsequently less expensive; nevertheless, examples of excellent quality do bring a premium price.

**Foil**-decorated enamels have metallic foil paillons (small shapes and dots) laid over colored enamel, with a clear enamel overcoating. This was almost exclusively a nineteenth century technique. The two buttons shown, with silver and gold foil paillons, are mounted in metal with cut steel (left) and paste (right) borders.

Perhaps the most coveted enamels are those in the **plique-à-jour** (light-of-day) technique. Like stained glass windows, they have no base, only transparent enamel between metal supports. The best examples have hand-assembled frames; others, like those pictured, have stamped, pierced metal frames. All are very rare.

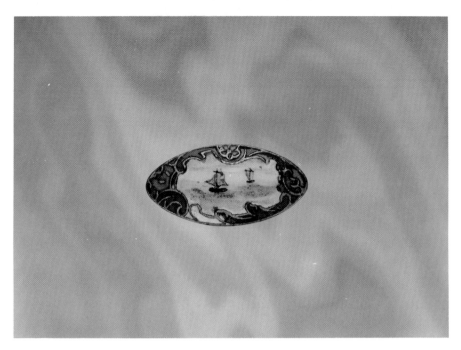

**Emaux-peints** (painted enamels) are most commonly found with floral designs; examples with people, animals, or scenes are therefore more valued by collectors. The little oval marine scene is unusual for its shape and subject. The border is champlevé enameling.

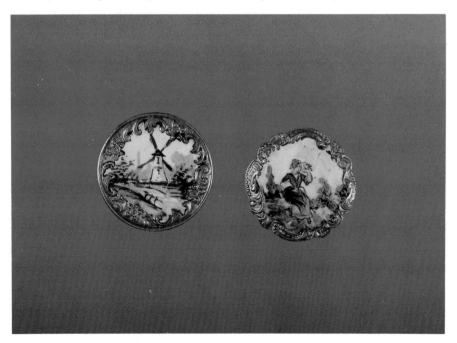

Two very desirable painted-enamel buttons with rococo brass borders. Neither is a common subject and both date from the mid-nineteenth century, most likely from France.

A very rare eighteenth century *en-grisaille* enamel button. *En-grisaille* is a difficult and long passé technique of painting in white and black shaded tones.

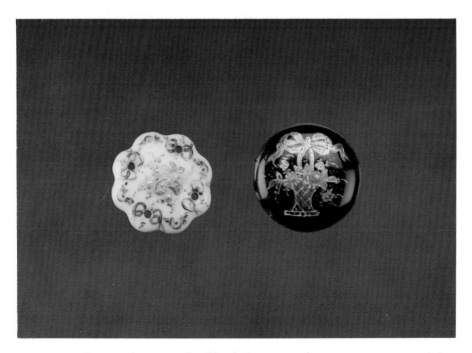

Emaux-peints buttons of copper with gold and silver paints, these were counter-enameled on the back for added strength. They date from the fin-du-siécle period.

Simply breathtaking, this is a rare black enameled button with foil foliage and a painted enamel cherub, beautifully executed with slight dimensionality.

Extremely rare and very valuable, these **Battersea-type** buttons are tiny works of pastoral art —enamel miniatures executed on ceramic buttons. They almost certainly date from the middle of the eighteenth century.

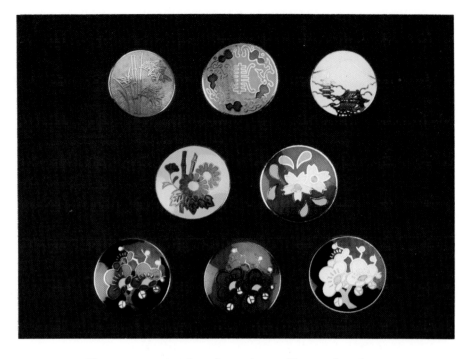

This is a group of modern cloisonné enamel buttons from Japan.

Modern enamels from the Far East, the top two buttons were made about 1950 in the Deccan, (the center for enamelwork in India) in the baisse-taille and champlevé methods on sterling. The button in the center of the group is from Siam (champlevé on brass), and the bottom two buttons are from Japan, ca. 1975.

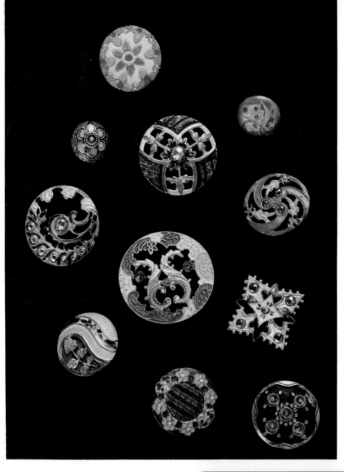

Easily confused with enamels, these buttons are painted, and very fragile! The paint easily chips, washes, and wears off; few are found in good condition. Although not valuable, painted buttons are quite pretty. They were produced through the Edwardian period until about 1920, and sometimes have Czechoslovakian back marks. The middle, top and bottom center buttons have embroidered fabric centers.

**Fabric** buttons all pre-1920: at the top is an eighteenth century button with silver wire-wrapped silk threads; at the center is a large and rare ribbon and embroidery button of the late-eighteenth or early-nineteenth century. The remaining fabric buttons include beaded, hand-painted, crocheted, and mounted in steel varieties. Unless a fabric button is very odd, funny, or gorgeous, little interest is shown for it. The eighteenth-century fabric buttons are under-valued today for their age and beautiful workmanship.

Can't you just imagine the Edwardian lady who first wore these quietly elegant, woven silk buttons?

Assorted modern fabric buttons including embroidered, sequined, painted, and beaded styles. The painted faces at top right are ca. 1920 garter buttons and very desirable.

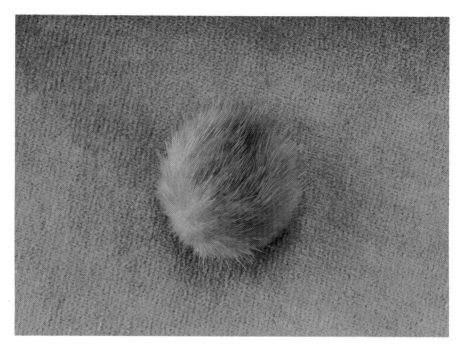

With the vast numbers of fur coats sold during this century, you'd expect to see more **fur** buttons, but they either stayed on the coats or non-fur buttons were used, for few are found. This one is mink.

**Goldstone** is a glittering mineral with copper inclusions that was quite popular in the jewelry trade in the nineteenth century. This unusual sew-through button was carved from the mineral goldstone and, being stone, is cold to the touch. Goldstone glass (aventurine) sparkles, but doesn't have the hard glitter of the stone. (The glass is far commoner.)

From about 1840 to 1870, glass factories in Bohemia, benefitting from increasing industrialization, produced vast quantities of small, hand-worked molded **glass** buttons in various colors and shapes.

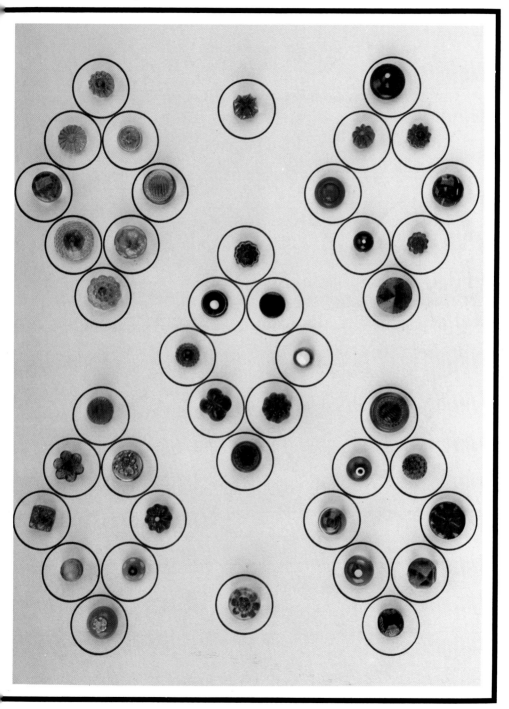

"Radiants" are a specialized type of early molded-glass button with transparent bodies and a dab of colored glass "tipped in" at the point where the metal shanks enter the backs. The radiating color effect is due to the natural magnification and distortion of glass. Each shape has its own name: glory, dewdrop, reflector, and so on. The top button is unusual: it's made of transparent vaseline glass; radiants with colored bodies are hard to find. (Pictured double their actual size.)

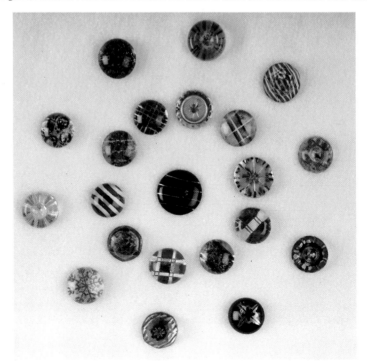

Lacy glass examples from the late-nineteenth-century are among the prettiest of buttons. Usually large, these transparent glass buttons had painted backs covered with a protective coating of silver paint, rather like a looking glass. Early collectors, who often scratched this off, preferred them clear, wanting to connect the buttons with the lacy patterned glass made by the Boston and Sandwich Glass Company of Massachusetts. No connection has ever been proven, although there are certainly great similarities in the patterns. Buttons in original condition are quite elusive and increasingly expensive.

---

**Opposite page:**
"Kaleidoscopes," almost always small in size, are buttons with glass bodies that are foiled and painted on the bottom. To protect the fragile design, a metal base plate with a shank soldered to it was glued on. These buttons are not mounted in metal, for the metal is simply under, not around, the glass. Unusual molded tops and larger sizes are particularly desirable. These buttons need gentle care.

Small, clear red "cranberry glass" buttons were quite popular in Victorian times, as evidenced by the great variety found in today's collections.

These small, molded glass buttons colored blue, amber, mottled tortoise, and tan-from the middle of the nineteenth-century, are far harder to find than are the cranberry glass or black glass buttons of the same size and subjects.

"Line designs" were formerly known in button circles as Victorian glass buttons. They were made at the end of the nineteenth century in many molded patterns and colors. Nearly always medium-sized, they were never actually pictorial except for the floral designs and the bow seen at the top in this photograph. (A great number of these buttons feature wonderful Art Nouveau-style designs, but none are included in this picture.)

Often called the aristocrats of glass buttons, "paperweight buttons" are a study unto themselves. It is possible to find paperweight buttons in all of the same techniques used in the larger, desk-size paperweights. A paperweight must have three parts—a crystal cap, a base, and a set-up (the decorative interior motif)—all permanently fused into one solid ball of crystal; paperweight buttons must also have, in addition, a sewing shank. Antique paperweight buttons always have metal loop shanks embedded in the backs. Modern paperweight buttons have either embedded or glued shanks.

These antique glass paperweight buttons from the 1840 to 1870 period include filigree, single-cane centers, bubble-balls, foil inclusions, and twisted spiral cane set-ups.

On the left is a peacock's-eye glass button: it's the green/blue coloring that determines the "peacock's-eye" nomenclature. This example is also a paperweight, but not all of them are. The two paperweight buttons on the right are very rare. Early fruit designs, such as that shown here, are tied with antique sulphides as the rarest paperweight-button styles. Also quite rare is the double rose paperweight on camphor glass; roses are ubiquitous in later paperweights, but such floral styles were almost unknown when this early example was created (ca. 1845).

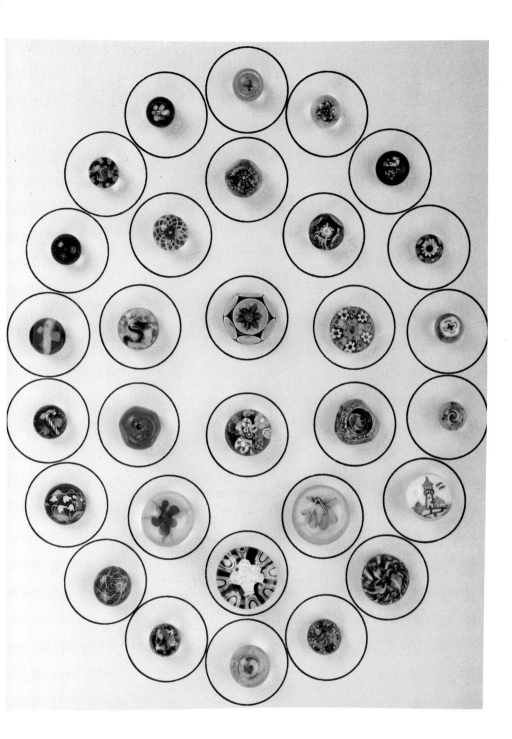

This fine collection of modern studio paperweight buttons, created since 1940, includes examples by such well-known glass artists as Charles Kaziun, Ronald Hansen, Ray Banford, William Iorio, and so on.

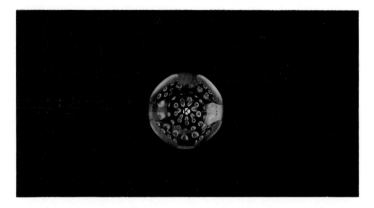

This signed, patterned-millefiori paperweight button with a transparent, faceted, green-glass casing was made by the late Charles Kaziun of Massachusetts, who was often acknowledged as the best desk paperweight artist in the world. His earliest paperweights were all buttons.

A truly lovely, large, double-overlay, faceted poinsettia paperweight button by Robert Hansen, son of the late Ronald Hansen, of Michigan. Ca. 1980

A large sulphide paperweight button by the late Theresa Rarig of Kansas who rediscovered the supposedly lost art of sulphide inclusions. Her sulphides varied greatly in quality; this button exemplifies her better work.

This example of the truly wonderful work done by Canadian glass-artist John Gooderham—who has made a vast array of buttons for collectors since the mid-1970s—demonstrates his technical skill, which is nearly perfect. He excels in the difficult technique of glass overlays, as seen here, and often works in extreme miniature: the faceted, double-overlay, gold-foil lovebird paperweight pictured here is enlarged. (It actually measures less than ¼" in diameter!)

As glass artists discover the world of buttons, more and more of them try their hand at paperweight buttons. Most of them find the small-scale work too challenging and problematic, but now and then, a new artist succeeds, to the delight of collectors. This example is by Will Stokes of Bellingham, Washington, whose buttons feature lamp-worked set-ups of extraordinary complexity. *Courtesy William Stokes, Blue Flame Studios.*

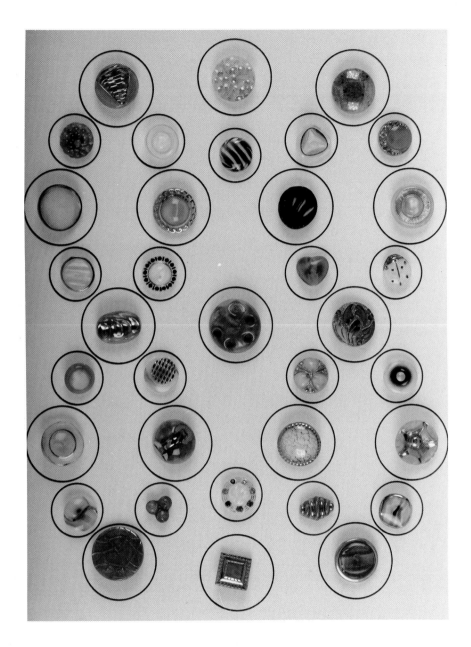

Starting about 1990, there began an absolute rage among button collectors for the West German glass buttons known as "moonglows." Produced in the 1950s and early 1960s, they were exported in huge quantities by large button firms, most notably B. Blumenthal and Company, Inc. The glass bodies of moonglow buttons have a shimmery cat's-eye finish covered by a thin layer of clear glass. That finish, showing through the top layer, defines a moonglow; everything else about them varies: size, shape, color, and trim.

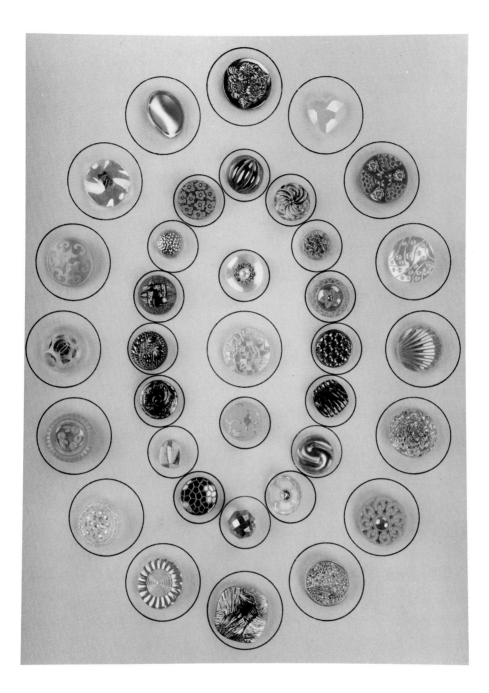

From the late 1950s and throughout the 1960s, West German glass companies produced iridescent, brash-colored "Aurora borealis" buttons, named for the natural light phenomenon of the same name. Ignored by most collectors until the 1990s, the Auroras have since soared in popularity.

Many clear glass buttons have been produced during the twentieth century. The majority were molded, but those pictured here were hand-cut from heavy crystal and have very sharp facets and edges.

Modern painted-back buttons from Czechoslovakia before World War II and from Germany after. The patterns are molded on the backs, then painted by hand. The four buttons at the top and at the bottom have a coating of contrasting paint covering the entire back. The large size of the center button is quite unusual.

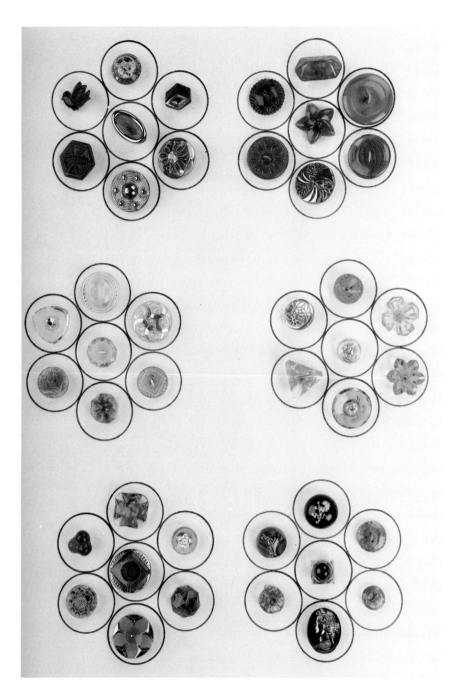

This assortment of twentieth-century clear glass buttons is mounted by color. (Mounting is a collector's term. It simply refers to groups of buttons that have been neatly attached to heavy cardboard, for purposes of display and competition. Button dealers often sell patterned cardboards, although some collectors cut the boards themselves and draw their own designs. Most collectors attach buttons to the mounting boards with short-lengths of plastic-coated wire. Early collectors used pipe-cleaners, but they often rusted, ruining many of the buttons with which they were in contact.)

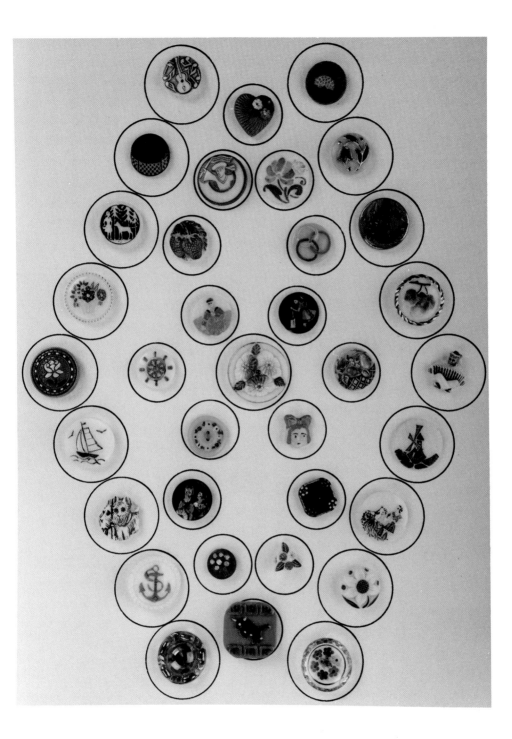

These mid-twentieth century opaque glass buttons have hand-painted trim.

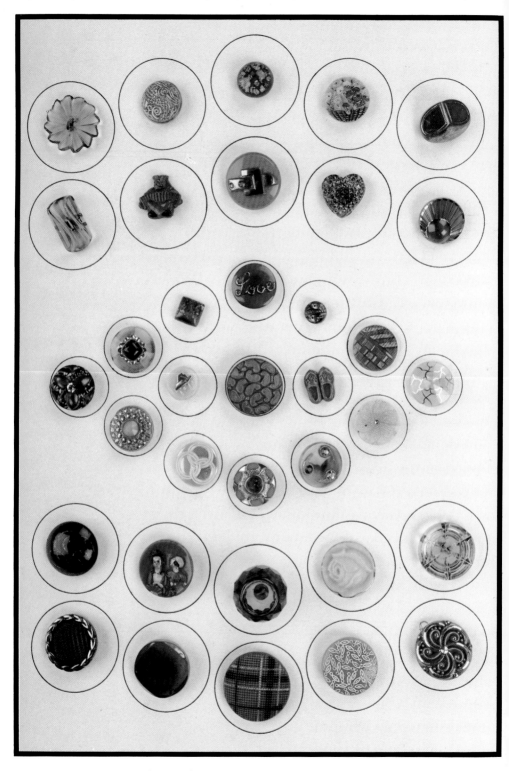

These modern glass buttons are grouped by color.

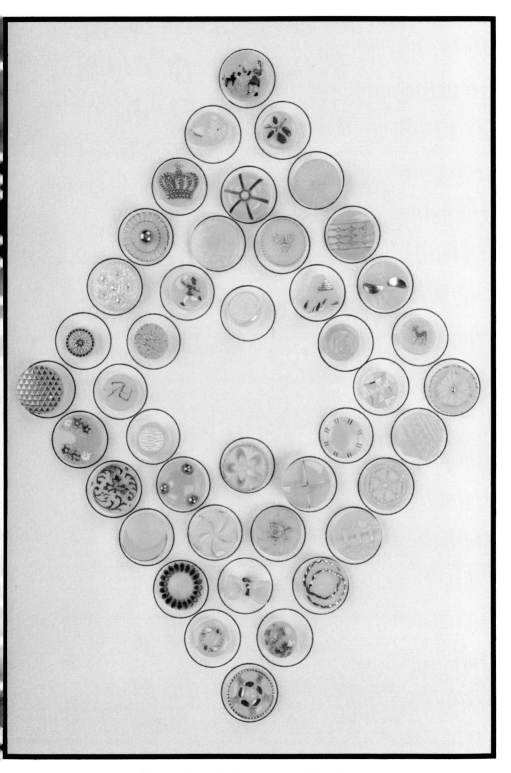

More modern glass buttons grouped by color.

**Hemp** roping is woven over this button into a cross design. This is a far more sturdy construction than the fabric buttons it resembles.

**Horn** buttons were made from the hooves and horns of cattle, buffalo, and similar work animals in Africa, Europe, and North and South America throughout the nineteenth century, and to a lesser degree in the twentieth century. Horn was sometimes used in its natural state by being cut into discs or carved into balls, but it was more often transformed with sufficient heat and pressure into a plastic (malleable) state, then die-stamped or molded. The majority of horn buttons were dyed black, although the natural horn colors, which range from amber to deep brown, are also found. A few molded horn buttons were dyed red; fewer still were green. Painted or lustred finishes are rarely found.

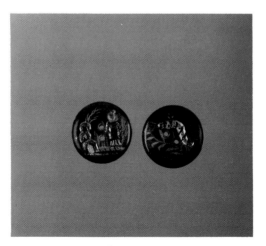

Two naturally-colored **horn** buttons with hand-painted scenes in a technique known as "encrusted"—the design is raised or built up with gesso-like material under paint or gilt. Made before the middle of the nineteenth century, such paintings are easily damaged.

Horn buttons with a variety of construction techniques and decor: the large, natural horn wolf's head is beautifully hand-carved in cameo, an extremely unusual technique for this material. The stars in the top button are inlaid; the stars on the "sew-through" at left are applied (riveted) cut steels. The green horn button has gold lustre on the raised, stamped areas, and the molded bottom button has a painted finish; both of these finishes are seldom seen on horn. The molded button at lower center is inlaid with tiny pearl discs.

Stamped and molded horn buttons with profile heads, in both natural and dyed coloring. The top right and far right buttons are centered with brass escutcheons in the shape of heads.

Horn buttons, including two Victorian molded and dyed examples with pearl and brass inlays and two modern African buttons carved from natural horn.

Buttons have been made with many different types of **inlays** in any number of materials, ranging from the most elegant —the glass micro-mosaics of Italy, fine piqué work in tortoise shell, and Shibayama-type inlays in ivory from Japan—to the somewhat crude, present-day Tibetan inlays in bone.

**Inlays** in horn buttons. Many different inlay materials and assorted techniques have been used to vary the naturally dull look of horn. These were made throughout the entire nineteenth-century.

**Ivory** was put to many uses in eighteenth and nineteenth-century buttons. During the twentieth century, although quite a few buttons have been custom-made for designers or carved for tourists, there has been very little commercial use of ivory for buttons. Ivory has been imitated by celluloid, plastic, and bone, and can best be identified by ruling out the others: plastic and celluloid can be pierced with a hot needle; bone has a coarse grain, a stringy, porous look in carved or cut areas, and is often riddled with tiny black specks (use a magnifier). Ivory has no inclusions or specks in it, is smooth, and usually has a cross-hatching or honeycomb pattern in the grain which may be apparent on just a small part of the surface. The grain is never raised or porous. Ivory has a soft look, whether polished to a high gloss or a mellow glow, and can be carved, painted, etched, and stained. True ivory buttons are almost always quite special.

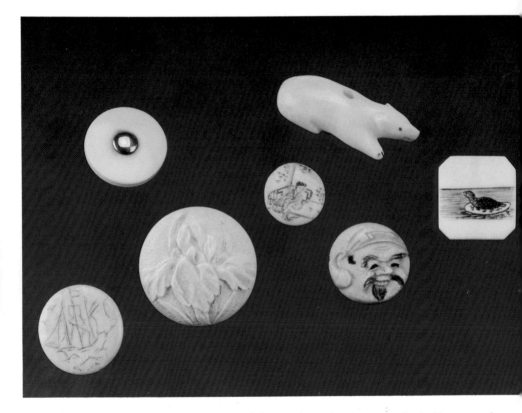

These ivory buttons include, at the upper left, an eighteenth-century pin-shanked button, and, at the lower left, a very rare antique scrimshaw button with an etched whaling ship design, from the early nineteenth century. Next to the scrimshaw is a *fin-du-siecle* carved iris from France. The polar bear was made ca. 1920-1940 by an Eskimo artist, and the square button is from Alaska. The two buttons in the center are Japanese; the upper one dates from the late Victorian period and the button with the face, ca. 1940.

**Jade** buttons have been made in China since the 1200s, but were at their height of popularity during the 1600s and early 1700s. Chinese jades of all types, including buttons of great antiquity, were stolen *en masse* during the looting of Peking following the fall of the last dynasty (1914), and brought to Europe. After many years of isolationism, the Chinese government has resumed trade relations with the west and opened its borders to tourists. Small numbers of wonderful old jades have again been brought out of China as families in need of money bring their inherited treasures to sell at the Canton foreign market (a large open-air bazaar). Old jade buttons are vastly under-rated (and under-priced) by button collectors, who are generally quite unaware of the true age and desirability of such pieces; on the other hand, they are held in great esteem by Oriental art and antiquities dealers and collectors.

There is something wonderful about the feel of a **jade** button—holding one is like touching the past. These buttons from China include a white jade cicada, an etched and cameo-cut pearl mounted in jade, a spinach green sew-through, and a very large, pierced chrysanthemum design. Except for the pearl-centered one—a Victorian-era example—these were carved no later than the 1700s.

Mourning had been a social custom throughout the eighteenth century, but it wasn't until the nineteenth century that it became so dramatized, and rigidly ruled. In England, not only was the death of Queen Victoria's prince consort, Albert, a cause for prolonged national mourning, but it was customary for each family to conduct personal mourning when a relative died. Diseases and wars kept the European continent in a semi-permanent state of mourning. In America, the Civil War and subsequent assasination of President Lincoln, followed by the Indian uprisings, added to the need for black jewelry, clothing, and buttons.

When Queen Victoria went into mourning, she chose **jet** for her personal accessories, and in so-doing gave an enormous boost to the jet-mining industry. Jet is a mineral, related to coal, mined in the Whitby area of England. The enormous demand for jet trim, jewelry, and buttons exceeded the supply. Jet also had to be hand-tooled or carved. A good substitute was found in black glass, a material that could be produced in endless quantity and efficiently manufactured with machines. Thus, the black glass industry was sent into high gear.

One should not expect to find genuine jet buttons; they simply don't exist beyond museums or rare collections. And yet, the author was told this when a new collector and found one anyway. You could be lucky, too!

This is a true **jet** button. True jet is easy to distinguish from black glass because it is carved, not molded, and can easily be cut with a sharp blade. Jet is lightweight in relation to its size; glass is heavy. Jet polishes to a soft gleam; glass can gleam, but usually has a glare or shine.

Today, black glass buttons are almost always referred to as jet by well-meaning, but uninformed, people. This original card of molded, black glass buttons is clearly, and erroneously, labeled "Genuine Jet". (The wording "Germany U.S. Zone" indicates the origin as 1945 to 1949.) Is it any wonder that it can be hard to convince people that black glass isn't jet?

Jeweled (containing genuine gem-quality stones) buttons are certainly exciting to find but unfortunately, that doesn't happen often. In the 1500s and 1600s, royalty often had huge numbers of jeweled buttons on one outfit. More trimming than fasteners, they were sewn up and down the legs and sleeves, around the waistline, and so on. Very few pre-eighteenth century jeweled buttons have survived.

This beautiful button is open-worked silver set with rubies and true oriental pearls; the origin is unknown but the workmanship and design suggest that it was made prior to the 1700s.

These buttons are gilded silver set with garnets, emeralds, mother-of pearl and true pearls. They have goldsmith's marks indicating their town of origin and date marks on the shanks. Austro-Hungarian region, ca. mid-nineteenth century.

**Lapis lazuli** isn't often seen in buttons; nevertheless, there are examples to be found. This lapis ball with a gold shank is a European nineteenth-century goodie, while the Chinese filigree-silver and copper button mounted with lapis is from the early twentieth century. Lapis lazuli is an opaque, semi-precious stone of deep blue color with small copper inclusions.

These modern **leather** buttons have raised figures. The leather was stamped from the back and tightly folded around a button base. In metal, the technique would be called répoussé. Their pictures make these buttons interesting even though they are quite recent.

Leather was used for relatively few buttons before the twentieth century. Nineteenth-century examples are usually similar to large pictures—die-stamped with various scenes and mounted— often in wood. The center button in this picture is modern.

**Linoleum** is an odd material for buttons. These designs painted on linoleum came from Mexico in the 1940s. They aren't easy to find.

The earliest **lithographed** buttons, with designs printed in black on white paper, were protected only with a coat of varnish before being set into metal mountings. Both of the buttons shown here have threadbacks (see shank types in Chapter 2). Because their date of origin coincides with the early nineteenth-century vogue for neo-classic art and images, the first lithographed buttons bear classically inspired designs.

By the last quarter of the nineteenth century, the art of lithography had so far developed that for the first time in history, beautifully colored prints were widely available. In the 1890s, lithographed buttons featuring heads of historical figures associated with the centennial of the French Revolution were popular (note the *fleur-de-lis* border on the left button); far fewer had scenes. Lithographed buttons of this era had protective clear celluloid covers.

In England, late in the nineteenth century, men's waistcoat-button sets often featured lithographed scenes, animals, sports themes, or beautiful ladies. Pictured here are two of the famous theatrical beauties of the era; below them are lithographed copies of famous paintings.

**Lucite** (a trademarked plastic of the DuPont Chemical Company) and other similar acrylic thermo-plastics were made into buttons from the late 1940s through the 1950s. These buttons demonstrate a surprising range of decorative techniques and subjects. In the group shown here, the top button has a celluloid head to create an unusual combination of materials. The leaf shape is a realistic, and examples of encased florals, and reverse-carved and painted florals are also shown. The two buttons in the bottom row are alike, but the color change gives them very different looks.

**Metal** buttons are found in wide variety. Eighteenth-century metal buttons were rather evenly divided between pewter, brass, silver, copper, and tombac, but by the nineteenth-century, brass button production far outstripped the rest. Metal buttons were die-stamped, engraved, molded, dyed, punched, and etched; many were further embellished with assorted trims.

**Aluminum** was worth a fortune when the button at right was made, around 1860. First seen by the public at the Paris exposition of 1855, aluminum was then a status material, more expensive than silver or gold; indeed, French Emperor Napoleon III replaced the royal silver flatware with a set made from the new "miracle metal." By the century's end, new mining and manufacturing techniques had made it a common metal and aluminum products plummeted in quality and value, as indicated by the smaller button, ca. 1900. Old aluminum buttons are not often found.

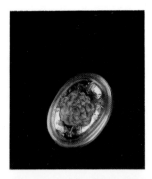

Here is a rare, solid **gold** button. Although not made in quantity, one does turn up from time to time. This is a man's waistcoat button -quite heavy for its size—with a beautiful Limoges-type, painted enamel chrysanthemum.

There were several different techniques and steps involved in the manufacture of this **brass** button: after it was cast, a separate, hand-tooled vine was hammered on, the cut-steel trim riveted in, the eyes hand-punched, and the "fur" engraved.

**Gold-plated** brass buttons—worn by men from the early to mid-nineteenth century—were a staple of the industry in America and England, and to a lesser degree in Germany. Often back-marked with a manufacturer's name and quality marks (such as triple gilt, rich orange, extra fine), these superbly-made, one or two-piece "Golden Age" buttons were die-stamped, then gold plated. In many cases, they were finished with fine hand-chased or punched detailing. In the center of the picture is an example of the best of this genre, a Golden Age "watchcase" button—named for its resemblance to the era's beautifully wrought gold pocket-watches—with complex engine-turned engraving and broad, beveled edges.

**Copper** was more prevalent in eighteenth-century button manufacture than at any time since, although this doesn't mean that these early copper examples are easy to find! Often called "colonials" by collectors (a reference to their age, not place of origin), these were large one-piece buttons with sturdy loop shanks. Most commonly embellished with hand-engraved designs, deluxe examples had enamel trim (see the button at the bottom), reverse-glass paintings laid in the centers, and so on. The oval button at the top is unusual for both its shape and smaller size; the feather and flower are more desirable than the usual non-pictorial (conventional) designs.

Copper picture buttons from the nineteenth century are uncommon; this large rooster design is particularly so.

**Cast iron** buttons of any sort are rare, but these, from the early nineteenth-century iron foundries of Berlin, are particularly so. During the long, financially devastating Franco-prussian wars against Napoleon, the German government asked its citizens to turn in their jewels and gold for the national treasury; in return they were given iron jewelry, produced for the cause at local foundries. All Berlin iron jewelry is cherished today. Buttons are perhaps the least encountered.

During the eighteenth century, one-piece cast **pewter** buttons were made in both Europe and the American colonies by small firms as well as individual pewterers. Pictured here are four examples: a ball-shaped button with a rose design and three early, signed American pewter buttons. The pewter button at the bottom is a fooler—it is faced (covered on the front only) with copper.

Pewter buttons can vary widely in appearance; these all are nineteenth-century, "bright-cut pewters" which were dyed in different colors before being engraved.

Throughout the 1960s and 1970s, large numbers of pewter buttons were made in Norway. First appearing on ski-sweaters, they later were exported for general use. Many are marked *Norge* (Norway) on the backs and feature snow-related designs such as snowflakes, skiiers, elk, reindeer, Vikings, and so on.

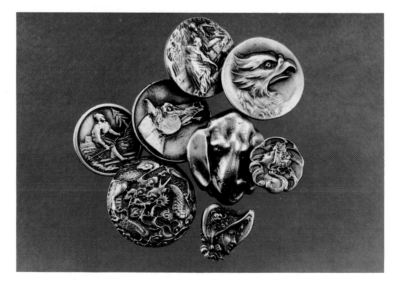

These wonderful pewter buttons by Battersea, Ltd., were produced late in the 1970s; they were ahead of their time for there was little public interest then for artistic, high quality buttons. Button collectors—busy chasing after antique buttons—practically ignored them as well. Now Battersea pewter buttons are hard to find and rapidly rising in price. (See Chapter 2 for Battersea shanks. It's worth a look, honest!)

If Battersea was just ahead of the button boom, the Danforth Pewterers were right on time. In the mid-1980s, buttons began to explode upon the fashion scene, and there was soon a tremendous increase in the public's interest in buttons. Danforth, a respected pewter tableware firm, had just begun to manufacture a very creative line of buttons in realistic shapes, marketing them under the (no longer used) label "Maiden Vermont". Sold through fabric and gift shops, the buttons have been a great success, with new designs being added regularly. These buttons are always backmarked with the company name or initials, and dated.

Of all the metals used for buttons, **silver** has perhaps the longest history and the most variety. There are more pre-eighteenth century silver buttons extant—from areas all over the world -than there are early buttons of all other materials combined. This fact, however, does not mean that very old silver buttons are commonly found; on the contrary, they are rare. Nevertheless, the possibility exists that the silver button you have may be very old indeed.

The large button shown here is very early, perhaps 1600, and probably had a Judaic origin. It was formed from a heavy sheet of silver, hammered out in répoussé, then rolled into this shape and almost invisibly joined along the seam; it was then decoratively pierced. Highly unusual; this button has two very odd shanks, each formed from a solid ball of silver that was drilled, hollowed out, and hammered into shape.

The Buddha button is Tibetan, pre-eighteenth century, cast in silver and crudely hand-punched to form an aureole (halo) around the deity. The other silver button, with a Buddhist stupa (shrine) symbol is much more recent, perhaps less than a century old.

These are typical cast-silver buttons made throughout Europe in the 1600s and 1700s. Hallmarks indicate that the top button is Belgian from the late 1600s; the bottom button has a French town-mark from the eighteenth century.

Filigree silver buttons are nearly impossible to date. They have been made with the same techniques for more than 300 years throughout Europe, the Middle East, and the Far East (where they continued to be produced in the 1950s.) Shown at the upper left is a pretty filigree silver button that probably is rather modern. The top button is definitely an antique and the matched pair at the right in a sleeve and a coat size are probably peasant work from the nineteenth century. The finest filigree in this group is the largest buton, which probably dates from the early 1800s.

**Opposite page:**
Hallmarked silver buttons are very popular. Their makers and city and date of origin can be exactly determined from the standardized system of markings found on the backs, shanks, or fronts. (When hallmarks are worked into the front design, they can be really hard to see.) An amazingly high percentage of hallmarked silver buttons were made within a four-year span at the turn of the twentieth century, in a myriad of pictorial subjects. Always well-designed and of quality manufacture, most hallmarked silver buttons are of English origin. Complete matching sets—in their original presentation boxes—can be found, particularly from English dealers. The button in the upper left corner of this group is rather odd: it has a perfectly plain face decorated with nothing but a hallmark.

Southwest American-Indian silver buttons have been made, particularly by Navajos, since the late 1800s. In the 1920s, when the automobile enabled tourists to first penetrate their remote homelands, these buttons began to be distributed outside the reservations. Popular fashion for Indian jewelry has ebbed and peaked a number of times since, but generally the heavier buttons made before the 1950s are preferred.

---

In the eighteenth century, faceted pieces of **cut steel** were riveted onto large, flat steel buttons as substitutes for the glitter of paste or jewels. Cut-steel trim on eighteenth-century buttons is usually much larger than similar trim on later ones. **Steel** was also rolled, cut-out, stamped, and combined with other materials. Blued-steel was popular during the Victorian-era, and examples of etched, stained, or painted steel buttons usually from France are worth the search.

Steel buttons rust easily. Cleaning products that remove rust also remove the shine and the buttons never look the same again. Keep them dry!

This star-shaped button was punched from a sheet of steel. Such oddly-shaped, very early nineteenth-century steels are elusive little buttons.

Court-steel buttons are named for the courtiers of England's King George III, who wore this style of button at court very early in the 1800s. The steel industry was centered in Birmingham, England at that time, and there were never before—nor since—steel buttons of such fine workmanship. Court-steel buttons often have well over a hundred tiny faceted-steel bits riveted on (to a steel base) by hand; the bottom one has 161 individual pieces.

Riveted cut-steels appeared on brass buttons by 1830. The quality does not approach that of the earlier (all-steel) examples, yet these are still attractive and were made with labor-intensive techniques: steel buttons from the end of the nineteenth-century, and their white-metal copies, are often simply stamped imitations. Buttons with applied cut-steels have rivets showing on the underside.

**Tin** buttons are not common; these are known as "crystallized tin" and date from the late-nineteenth century. First lacquered in a dark color, a design was etched through the color to the tin base, which then reflected a frosty, silvery image.

**Tôleware** buttons have decorations painted on lacquered or japanned brass bases. They are often found damaged, but when in good condition, they are very attractive and currently not particularly expensive. In view of their age (from the nineteenth century), relative scarcity, and hand-painted workmanship, tôleware buttons seem to have good investment potential today.

This unusual metal is **tombac**, an alloy of copper and zinc with a soft grey/white gleam that shines between the radiances of silver and pewter. Tombac buttons, made only during the eighteenth century, aren't magnetic. They usually have a peculiar, cone-shaped metal mound at the base of the shank. (This is not, however, an infallible method of identification; a very few copper and brass pre-1800 buttons also have "cone-shanks".)

**White metal** buttons from the twentieth century are numerous and made from assorted mixtures of metal substances. One large group made in France in the forties and fifties are known as "French-whites." These are of one-piece construction, in large or medium sizes and depict interesting subjects, sometimes copied from old buttons or medallions. They have a pewter-like appearance but are lighter in weight, and have a distinctive white sheen. They don't command the price of older picture buttons unless the subject is really desirable. They were often sold in sets, such as the "ethnic headdresses of Europe" or "great composers of the world."

**Nuts** have been pictured on buttons and buttons have been shaped like nuts, but few real nuts have been turned into buttons. This hazel nut was probably a manufactured example, rather than a homemade button, since it appears to have a commercial shank. (A group of buttons truly made from nuts—tagua or corozo—is shown under the vegetable ivory heading.)

**Onyx** buttons of the type pictured were carved in Mexico, most of them in the 1940s and 1950s. In the nineteenth century, men sometimes wore elegant, black onyx mourning buttons.

**Papiér-mâché** was a craft material that became a Victorian mania and so it was natural that it was used to make buttons. Decorations include pearl inlay (on the top button), laminated pearl (on the bottom button), gilt, paint, and lacquer. These buttons usually have a shiny black-lacquered back with an inserted wire-loop shank; a few have carved self-shanks.

These large **mother-of-pearl** buttons, or, as collectors call them, "pearls", were of average quality for their time (1875-1930). Not of great intrinsic value, they are still of practical use and look beautiful on any garment.

Mother-of-pearl buttons are often beautifully crafted. The large ocean pearl button at the top is inlaid with birds cut from abalone shell and engraved. The button on the left shows a bird cut in high relief, etched with further details, and trimmed with cut steels. The button at the right shows a crane carved in cameo relief.

Mother-of-pearl buttons from the nineteenth century often were trimmed with metal: cut steel, tin watch-wheels, and brass escutcheons were the most popular. (Pictured smaller than actual size.)

Some of the very labor-intensive buttons of the past—little pearl cameos mounted in small metal buttons. The larger pearl cameo buttons are more desirable, but even the small ones, amazingly detailed for their size, are prized by button collectors. Cameo-carvings with animals, scenes, and people are the most sought after, but none are unappreciated, nor are they inexpensive, even in this small size.

These are sales cards with white and dyed pearls from the 1940s and 1950s. Note that the manufacturers have stressed "genuine pearl" on the cards; the various plastics were beginning to make serious inroads into the pearl button industry, and it was not long before the industry did indeed collapse.

**Plastic** buttons make up this assortment dating from 1950 to 1985 with rhinestone, cork, and brass trims. The clover design is an imitation of a glass paperweight. The various plastics made since 1945 are difficult to identify specifically, and in popular terminology they are grouped together as "hard plastics," including nylon, polyvinyl, and petro-chemical-based types. (The earlier plastics—celluloid, Bakelite, and Lucite—are categorized separately.)

Pierced pearl work was among the more difficult techniques for Victorian button carvers since the material is thick and brittle and the patterns were complex. Manufacturers usually had an experienced specialist to do this work. Note that on the buttons at the lower left and right, the piercings are pictorial, a house and a horse's head: this is rather unusual. The three, shaded-pearl buttons with steel trim were made in France during their Aesthetic period (ca. 1885) and are quite deluxe.

From what do you think these buttons are made? Silver, brass and pewter? No, they all are plastics, the easiest material with which to fool you! Manufactured from the late 1930s onward (the sun face button at the upper right was made in 1992), they each are electro-plated with a thin layer of metal. Their very light weight is one way to differentiate them from metal; also, plastic buttons almost always have a molded self-shank, not an added metal shank.

**Porcelain** buttons and **pottery** buttons are similar in their decorative techniques, age ranges, and overall appearance. The primary difference is found in their ceramic materials: porcelain is made with hard clay and fired to high temperatures while pottery is made with softer clay and fired to lower temperatures. Most porcelain buttons have molded self-shanks while most pottery buttons have inserted metal loop-shanks.

These **porcelain** buttons, decorated with transfer designs, were made throughout the nineteenth century. The black and white transfer designs are the earliest, from the beginning of the century; colored transfers followed within a decade. The fox is an early and rare button mounted in metal and was surely made for a hunting coat; it has additional highlighting in enamel paint over the transfer. Manufactured a bit later, around 1830, and particularly coveted, the largest button is illustrated with a scene from the Tortoise and the Hare fable, copied from a Doré etching. The buttons with the Oriental couple and the nesting birds also date from the early decades of the century. So does the jockey on the horse, a particularly desirable, yet unusual, subject. The button at the lower left in a pudding mold shape, and the image of Queen Louise of Prussia at the lower right are more recent, dating from the end of the Victorian age (ca. 1900). The button at the top, the little rose, is marked "Limoges, France," and is modern.

Arita porcelain buttons were made in Japan at least as early as the 1930s. They were sporadically exported by tourists before 1942, and commercially exported in limited numbers during the early 1960s. Arita porcelains came from the town of Arita, and were made by many different small family enterprises. They are made with an especially fine clay, found only in one particular location -a mountain next to the town. The buttons do not resemble the well-known Arita porcelain tablewares, but share their detailed molding and decorative techniques. Arita buttons enjoyed a marked increase in popularity in the early 1990s and a correspondingly rapid rise in price. Age alone doesn't determine the price of buttons!

Three modern porcelain buttons: the sailboat design on the left is painted by hand and mounted in brass while the two polychrome scenes are transfer-printed designs.

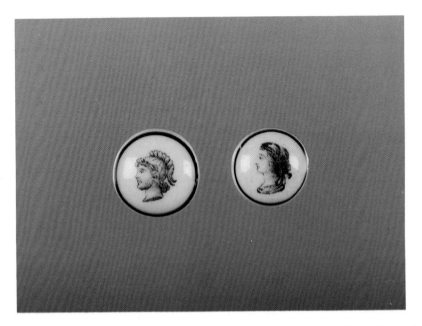

**Pottery** buttons with so-called "Liverpool" transfer decorations, so named after the English town where the technique was invented, date from the beginning to the middle of the nineteenth century. The early designs include neo-classical heads, such as these in black-on-white grounds. The similar buttons, often mounted in metal, with magenta-colored transfer heads on white ground, are thought to have been made in France during the same period.

The progression of the "Liverpool" transfer technique can be followed on buttons. The early black on white transfers were modified to the use of grey tones with shading added. Later, flat multi-colored images were made and, finally, fully dimensional designs with blended coloring. The buttons, often mounted in metal, pre-date 1860. Birds and animals are rarer than heads, but all are desirable.

Wedgwood pottery buttons were first made in the last quarter of the eighteenth century. Following the success of Josiah Wedgwood in developing his colored jasperware pottery, other firms imitated the technique. Because these buttons were seldom marked, their origin cannot be specified and they are usually referred to as jasperware (although many, are genuine Wedgwood products). Their production continued into the early nineteenth century, but not in large quantity. The Wedgwood firm also made buttons in the 1950s, for the first time in over a century. These were self-shanked, signed and dated, and came in two different designs.

A pin-shanked, American pottery button from the famed Norwalk pottery made early in the nineteenth century. This is an average example (though none are common), very typical of the work of this pottery. There are a number of far more unusual Norwalk buttons in collections.

Three eighteenth-century, Wedgwood-type jasperware buttons set in heavy mountings of silver, brass, and copper, respectively. All early jasperware buttons are valuable; rarities include odd shapes, tiny one-holed shirt buttons, and colors other than blue and white.

Almost every collector has a favorite type of button and for many it is the Satsuma pottery buttons of Japan. The antique ones with far better workmanship than the more-plentiful modern buttons are hard to find, but all Satsumas have become expensive. Shown here are late-nineteenth century Satsuma buttons of rare shapes (such as the little ball and the small star) and extraordinary decorations (the Greek-key bordered pair in particular). Many early Satsuma buttons are mounted in metal—usually copper or silver. All Satsuma buttons have a crackled glaze. To determine age, older ones have fine details, heavy use of gold paint or gilding, and an overall background pattern of tiny gold dots.

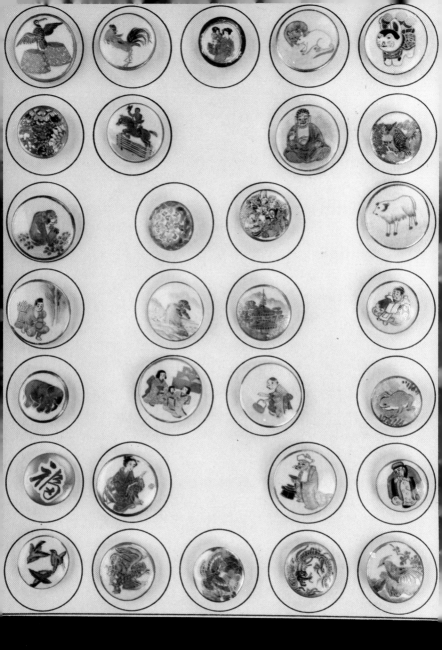

Modern Satsuma buttons, ca. 1950s, have less detailed design and coloring than the older ones, but nevertheless have great appeal for many collectors. The subject matter is myriad, and there are distinctly different levels of quality: some are beautifully decorated; others are not.

During the twentieth century, pottery buttons have been produced all over the world. This group of buttons from Indians of the American Southwest were made by potters from various pueblos including Acoma, Zia, and Hopi. They date from the 1940s and 1950s.

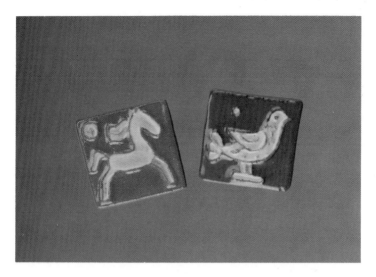

Modern pottery buttons from Denmark, ca. 1950.

Modern Delft pottery buttons from Holland with hand-painted designs. Each is marked on the back. The oddly-shaped button at the left has a molded self-shank while the other three buttons have glued-on metal shanks.

**Paste** (glass) jewels were used as a substitute for real gems in Europe as early as the 1700s. They were so effective that they became a status material themselves—even the wealthiest patrons wore them in profusion. Paste was often used as a border material on eighteenth-century buttons, and was the primary material of many later buttons before it was supplanted by rhinestones and later imitations. At the left is an early grain-set paste button in a fine, hand-worked, gold-plated mounting. At the right is an excellent quality, mid-nineteenth century, prong-set paste button.

**Quartz**, in a form known as tiger's-eye, a yellow-brown stone with an opalescent play of color from within. The button is modern, from a rock shop, ca.1970.

Although some people continue to use the old term "paste" for fake gems, these mid-twentieth century buttons are made with the later glass stones from eastern Europe known as **rhinestones**. At the left is a pavé (as in paved) button covered with rhinestones while the other buttons in the group have prong-set stones. The rhinestone buttons of this period (ca. 1925-1955) were of high quality, and hand-set.

**Rock crystal** buttons are few and far between. This small silver-mounted button, with red foil underneath the faceted rock crystal stone, was worn on a man's breeches in the early-eighteenth century. (Many collectors think that this type of button may actually date from the 1600s.)

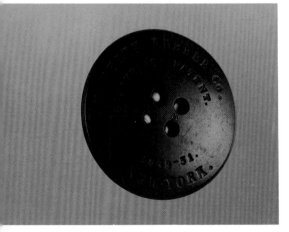

**Rubber** is the one material used for making buttons that could truly be called all-American. Soon after Charles Goodyear discovered the secret to making rubber a viable product in the mid-nineteenth century, there were molded rubber buttons on the market. Always backmarked, the buttons are usually black, with brown, orange, tan, and red-orange rarely found. Button shapes include squares, melons, balls, scallops, and 2-piece oddities. Most rubber buttons are reasonably priced, but watch out for the rarities, such as American Presidential political campaign buttons from 1868, which are scarce and very valuable. Rubber buttons can be a good category for a beginning collector since there is far more to them than may be readily apparent.

This is the rarest backmark found on rubber buttons: it reads "Novelty Rubber Co. Goodyear's patent. 1849-51. New-York." Most buttons are dated with just one year. There are so many variations of backmarks on rubber buttons that some collectors specialize in just that.

**Snakeskin** buttons became a minor fad in the 1920s, but since then have rarely sidled into the button world.

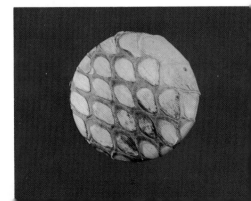

This prisoner-of-war button from the Napoleonic Wars (1800 -1815) is truly a tangible piece of history. The button was painstakingly fashioned from plaited **straw** and trimmed with a carved-coal cameo head of Bacchus. It was certainly a wishful thought for a prisoner to sculpt the wine-loving, womanizing god of revelry, don't you think?

These three straw and raffia buttons all date from the twentieth century; the larger one is interwoven with pine needles.

Photography was a new invention and still quite a novelty when these **tintype** buttons were made in the mid-nineteenth century. Mounted into little button frames, they were quite popular for men's vests; larger mountings are far more unusual. Tintypes fade and scratch easily, and should be kept covered, out of the sun. More women and children are pictured than men, and very few show two or more subjects. There were also tintype buttons that were not one-of-a-kind photos, but multiple prints of popular personalities, for example the famous Civil War generals, President Grant, and Queen Victoria. And sometimes the pictures aren't of real people at all, but are photographs of well-known paintings or lithographs.

True **tortoise shell** was used for limited numbers of buttons in the nineteenth century, and even fewer in the twentieth. Early examples are almost always inlaid with mother-of-pearl or brass, or—in the finest—gold and silver in a technique known as piqué-point. Chinese tortoise shell buttons were engraved or cameo-carved. The buttons in this group are modern. The one decorated with sterling silver is signed by William Spratling, an American jeweler in Taxco, Mexico during the 1930s and 1940s.

A large percent of the deluxe buttons from the eighteenth century, particularly the French ones, are known as **under-glass** buttons. They have a metal back and edge, and a glass cover protecting the central design. The interiors range from miniature paintings on ivory to tiny wax sculptures, to pressed flowers. Usually large in size, under-glass buttons were often custom-made by artists or jewelers. Shown here are two lovely pastoral paintings of fishermen, one on ivory and set in copper, and the other a gouache set in silver. Such buttons have been the best investments in the button world for they are the apex of button artistry and desirability.

Some under-glass buttons of the eighteenth and nineteenth centuries were painted with scenes on the reverse side of the glass cover. The reverse-paintings shown in this group range in date from the beginning of the 1800s (the fox-head) to the end (the impressionistic bird). The button at the top of the group is a gorgeous spaniel's head mounted in an ornately carved wooden button. At the bottom is a luminous painting of two pansies which is a German button that may actually pre-date the fox. Nineteenth-century reverse-painted buttons are surprisingly reasonable, in comparison with the under-glass buttons of the type in the previous photo. In some cases, the techniques are nearly the same and the buttons are only a couple of decades apart in age; they simply haven't been "discovered" yet.

**Vegetable ivory** is the meat of the Tagua or Corozo nut from South America. Although perhaps more vegetable ivory buttons were made between 1885 and 1920 than any other, most people today have never even heard of this material. The nuts grow in large clusters on Tagua palms. They were shipped to the United States, Japan, and Europe for decorating. Once the skin was peeled off, the material had an ivory color and a hard, close-grained structure reminiscent of true ivory. A button-maker's dream, it could be buffed, dyed, engraved, carved, pierced, embossed with dies, trimmed with other materials, and stencilled, but by the 1930s, it was superseded by celluloid and Bakelite.

As an ecological move, early in the 1990s, there began a drive to re-start the vegetable-ivory button trade. The Tagua palms grow in the rain forest area; rather than burn the trees to create cleared farmland, their nuts could once again become a "cash crop," saving the rain forests from further destruction.

A tagua nut (**vegetable ivory**).

Identification of vegetable ivory is easier from the back. The typical grain can be seen on the bottom buttons. The top and right buttons have characteristic pits known as "chatter-marks." Dyes did not penetrate beyond the first layer of this material: wherever a dyed button was cut, the original ivory color showed; therefore, when a dyed button was carved it was automatically bi-colored, a plus for manufacturers. It's also an aid to identifying this material. The sewing holes were drilled after the buttons were dyed and decorated; the dye didn't penetrate, so the original ivory color shows inside the holes.

Vegetable ivory decorating techniques: the nut's skin was sometimes left partially on for decorative effect, as in the face (its nose and hair) and the button with red paint. The leaf at the right was stencilled and the butterfly at left was embossed.

**Wood** buttons made during the nineteenth century very often had steel or brass decorations. The very large one at center has a separate border made of intricately carved little wooden beads strung tightly on an encircling wire.

**Yarn** embroidery buttons with wrapped yarn borders on cardboard and fabric bases. These wonderful embroideries, among the most attractive of modern fabric buttons, were sold at the New York World's Fair in 1939. Their country of origin is unknown.

These inlaid and laminated wooden buttons date from the 1940s on. The dark, rectangular button (upper right) is rosewood inlaid with ivory, from India.

# SOURCES

To join the National Button Society (and receive *The National Button Bulletin*), send $15.00 annual dues to Lois Pool, Secretary, 2733 Juno Place, Akron, Ohio 44333-4137.

Most states have a state button society and there are many local chapters scattered throughout the United States and Canada. Almost every state hosts its own button shows; the National Button Society also holds an annual week-long convention.

Many foreign countries have button dealers and collectors who are associated with the National Button Society. There is also a British Button Society; members receive *Button Lines*, a quarterly publication, and hold meetings twice annually.

# SUGGESTED READING

For general information on buttons and their manufacture, I highly recommend *The Collector's Encyclopedia of Buttons* by Sally Luscomb. Long out of print, this book was reprinted by Schiffer Publishing in 1992 and can be ordered from them at 77 Lower Valley Road, Atglen, Pennsylvania 19310, or from a bookstore.

For an excellent study of the art of the button (and a glimpse of some of the finest buttons in the world) read *Buttons* by Diana Epstein and Millicent Safro, published in 1991 by Harry N Abrams, Inc. N Y.

For the serious collector, *The Big Book of Buttons* -- the most comprehensive work on buttons and their history -- was also reprinted in 1991 . Appropriately named, this book describes an enormous number of buttons individually. Written by Elizabeth Hughes and Marion Lester and originally published privately in 1981, it was re-issued by New Leaf Publishers, (printed by J S McCarthy Co ) Augusta, Maine.

Many other button books have been privately published throughout the years and are out of print. The Secretary of the National Button Society keeps a list of people who have out of print books for sale. Contact Miss Lois Pool, Secretary, 2733 Juno Place, Akron, Ohio 44333-4137.

The best sources of information on buttons are the back issues of two magazines, *The National Button Bulletin* and *Just Buttons*. *Just Buttons* is no longer published, but for over 30 years it was a monthly joy for collectors. *The National Button Bulletin* is published 5 times a year by the National Button Society and is sent to all members of the society. Filled with informative articles, pictorial essays, and even a feature for junior members, it also contains information on various button shows and keeps members abreast of related events. Back issues of both magazines are sometimes available through button dealers.

For further information on paperweight buttons, see two articles in *Glass Collector's Digest*, one in the June/July 1992 issue and the other in August/September 1992, by Peggy Ann Osborne. Order back-issues from *Glass Collector's Digest*, Antique Publications, P.O. Box 553, Marietta, Ohio, or call them at 800-533-3433.

The following guide is intended only as a point of reference for new collectors to enable them to judge the relative desirability or rarity of the various types of buttons. It is in no way intended as a price list.

Prices in the button world are very unstable at this time. Experienced collectors and specialized button dealers have been shocked at the recent rise in the prices of many types of buttons. The extraordinary popularity of buttons throughout the collectible and antique fields has changed what was once a rather private community of knowledgeable collectors into an explosive seller's market. The public is buying buttons in droves, and from dealers who, new to the field, have no basis of knowledge on how to price their buttons. These new customers and dealers have contributed greatly to the rapid price increases. The price ranges suggested in this book are based on an average of what I think specialized button dealers would currently charge a button collector

Pricing will also vary by location: in the U.S., the East Coast prices are usually higher. Certain buttons are more valued in England and will cost more there than in the U.S.. Fine old French historical buttons are greatly valued in France, but may be a relative bargain elsewhere. Japanese collectors are at present paying premium prices for Satsumas, which are far from inexpensive in the U.S.

Particular types of buttons that fit into other collectible fields are often worth far more as collectibles in those specialties than they are as buttons: sports collectors pay more for sports related buttons than do button collectors, Bakelite collectors pay more for Bakelite buttons, Disney collectors value early Disney buttons, and so on.

Value ranges are in U.S. dollars. Positions of photographs on a page are indicated by the letter codes L (left), R (right), C (center), T (top) and B (bottom).

| Page | Position | Value Range |
|---|---|---|
| | L | 18-22 |
| | R | 10-12 |
| | | 2-15 |
| | T | 15-20 |
| | B | 5-8 |
| | T | .50-15 |
| | B | 4-25 |
| | | 2-8 (realistic insect shape would be considerably higher) |
| | T | .50-8 |
| | B | .50-6 |
| | T | 2-8 (the cigarette packs are higher, and rising) |
| | B | 2-9 |
| | T | 7-15 |
| | B | 15-55 |
| | | 8-15 |
| | T | 20-25 |
| | B | 2-4 |
| | T | 12-24 |
| | B | 12-18 |
| | T | 15-18 |
| | B | 20-35 |

| Page | Position | Value Range |
|---|---|---|
| 20 | T | 20-35 |
| 20 | B | 2-8 |
| 20 | C | 40-60 |
| 21 | T | 55-75 |
| 21 | C | 8-12 |
| 21 | B | 25-40 |
| 22 | T | 15-25 |
| 22 | C | 10-12 |
| 22 | B | 10-15 |
| 23 | T | 250-350 (medium sized) |
| 23 | C | 30-40 |
| 23 | B | 8-15 |
| 24 | T | 25-35 |
| 24 | C | 35-45 |
| 24 | B | 45-60 |
| 25 | T | 15-20 |
| 25 | C | 70-85 |
| 25 | B | 12-18 |
| 26 | T | 20-30 |
| 26 | B | 12-35 |
| 34 | | 12-20 (the whole card) |
| 35 | | 650-800 (for the pair) |
| 36 | | 85-125 |
| 37 | | 5-35 |
| 38 | T | 20-35 |
| 38 | B | 25-80 |
| 39 | T | 2-14 |

| Page | Position | Value Range |
|---|---|---|
| 39 | B | sold in sets of 9 at 85 and up; 11 each for singles |
| 40 | | 4-12 |
| 41 | | 4-10 |
| 42 | B | 2-4 |
| 43 | T | 14-18 |
| 43 | B | 20-30 to a button collector; far higher to a baseball or gambling collector |
| 44 | | 150-250 |
| 45 | | 12-20 |
| 46 | | 80-110 (fine quality in original case) |
| 47 | T | 30-50 |
| 47 | B | 1-3 each button |
| 50 | T | 10-12 |
| 50 | C | 5-35 |
| 50 | B | 1-2 |
| 51 | | 1-10 |
| 52 | T | 4-12 |
| 52 | B | 2-8 |
| 53 | | 1-18 |
| 54 | | 4-20 and 40-55 for the signed scrimshaw |

| Page | Pos | Value |
|---|---|---|
| 55 |  | 7-20 |
| 56 | T | 15-24 |
| 56 | B | 8-15 |
| 57 | T | 20-35 |
| 57 | B | 75-115 |
| 58 | T | 8-15 and 40-60 for the enamel |
| 58 | B | 40-60 (for set of two) |
| 59 | T | 15-25 |
| 59 | B | 25-30 |
| 60 | T | 14-16 each |
| 60 | B | 1 for the plain ones; 20-50 for the carved animals |
| 61 |  | 2-3 |
| 62 | T | 10-12; center one is 25-35 |
| 62 | B | 15-20 |
| 63 |  | 10-15; the clown 35-45 |
| 64 |  | 25-35; the seahorse 45-65 |
| 65 | T | 7-10 |
| 65 | B | 2-4 |
| 66 |  | 2-7 |
| 67 |  | 2-6 |
| 68 |  | 4-20 |
| 69 | T | 3-10 |
| 69 | B | 5-10; for the mosaic, a fine example in a rare subject matter: 75-125 |
| 70 | T | 4-10 |
| 70 | B | 4-10 |
| 71 | T | 3-15 |
| 71 | B | 3-5 |
| 72 | T | 1-4 |
| 73 | T | 1 for the plain sew-through; 4-15 for the rest |
| 73 | B | 10-12 |
| 74 |  | 20-30 for the large |
| 75 |  | 10-30 |
| 76 | T | 1-6 |
| 76 | B | 5-10 for the smaller; 30-70 in large sizes |
| 77 |  | 2-35 |
| 78 |  | average examples 3-5; Calicoes in rare patterns, medium-sized, or framed in |
| 79 |  | 1-3 |
| 80 | T | 15-25 |
| 80 | B | 1-8 |
| 81 | TL | 15-25 |
| 81 | TR | 3-5 |
| 81 | B | 10-20 |
| 82 |  | 30-40 |
| 83 | T | 20-25 |
| 83 | C | 200-250 each |
| 83 | B | 12-18 |
| 84 |  | 15-35 |
| 85 | T | 30-60 |
| 85 | B | the volatility of prices on this type of enamel, even in this lesser quality, preclude any present suggestion of value |
| 86 | T | 45-60 (the button shown is smaller than pictured; a large one, if found in this shape and subject matter, would be much more expensive) |
| 86 | B | 65-80 |
| 87 | T | 550-700 |
| 87 | B | 45-65 |
| 88 | T | 275-350 |
| 88 | B | 400 and up |
| 89 | T | 5-7 |
| 89 | B | 5-7 |
| 90 | T | 3-7 |
| 90 | B | 3-6; older and more unusual center button 15-25 |
| 91 | T | 2-5 |
| 91 | B | under 7, except the squirrel at 12 and the garter buttons at 40+ |
| 92 | T | 1 |
| 92 | B | 3-4 |
| 93 |  | 3-12 |
| 94 | T | 10-20 |
|  |  | metal (see top button) are far more expensive: 35-70 |
| 94 | B | 8-20 |
| 95 |  | 7-40 |
| 96 | T | 2-4 |
| 96 | B | 3-6 |
| 97 |  | 7-15 |
| 98 | T | 10-30 |
| 98 | B | 10-12 for peacock's eye; 35-45 for the others |
| 99 |  | 5-300: this highly specialized field has wide price variations between both types and individual artists, with Kaziun examples the most expensive (see p.162, Suggested Reading). |
| 100 | T | 200-300 |
| 100 | C | 75-100 |
| 100 | B | 20-30 |
| 101 | T | 50-80 |
| 101 | B | 35-50 |
| 102 |  | 4-12 |
| 103 |  | 3-10 |
| 104 |  | 2-8 |
| 105 |  | 3-14 |
| 106 |  | 2-14 |
| 107 |  | 2-8 |
| 108 |  | 2-7 |
| 109 |  | 2-6 |
| 110 | T | 2-5 |
| 110 | B | 6-10 |
| 111 |  | 4-15; the very unusual, large wolf's head cameo 80-90 |
| 112 | T | 4-10 |
| 112 | B | 4-12 |
| 113 |  | 4-20 |
| 114 |  | 8-60 |
| 115 |  | 35-75 |
| 116 |  | though not actually of any intrinsic value, true jet buttons are very rarely found; their value is |

| Page | Pos | Price |
|---|---|---|
| | | whatever an avid collector would pay |
| | T | 200-325 |
| | B | 80-150 |
| | T | 12-20 |
| | B | 4-7 |
| | T | 8-24 |
| | B | 5-10 |
| | T | 14-20 |
| | B | 30-50 |
| | T | 12-18 |
| | B | 8-20 |
| | | 1 & 25 |
| | T | 30-40 |
| | B | 45-65 |
| | | 2-10 |
| | | "watchcase" example at center 25-35 |
| | T | 20 for the smaller; others ranging 45-85 |
| | B | 55-75 |
| | T | Too rare to have a market price |
| | B | the rose 4-6; the rest 12-20 |
| | | 2-10; the largest ones 16-20 |
| | T | 2-7 |

| Page | Pos | Price |
|---|---|---|
| 128 | B | 10-18 |
| 129 | | 7-10 per card |
| 130 | | 100 and up |
| 131 | T | 30-45 |
| 131 | B | 30-45 |
| 132 | | 6-22 |
| 133 | | 30-80 |
| 134 | | 6-12 |
| 135 | TL | 40-50 |
| 135 | TR | 10-15 |
| 135 | B | 2-5 |
| 136 | T | 8-20 |
| 136 | B | 5-20 |
| 137 | T | 35-45 |
| 137 | B | 10-25 |
| 138 | T | 1 |
| 138 | C | 3-5 |
| 138 | B | 12-30 |
| 139 | | 3-7 |
| 140 | T | 50-70 |
| 140 | B | 2-12 |
| 141 | T | 15-30 |
| 142 | T | 2-30 |
| 142 | B | 2-6 |
| 143 | | 1-7 |
| 144 | | 10-325 (the most expensive by far are the jockey, quite a rarity, and the largest one) |
| 145 | L | 60-75 |
| 145 | B | 5-15 |

| Page | Pos | Price |
|---|---|---|
| 146 | T | 25-40 |
| 146 | B | 65-90 |
| 147 | L | 300-550 |
| 147 | R | 7-9 |
| 148 | | 40-250 |
| 149 | | 35-65 |
| 150 | | 12-25 |
| 151 | T | 5-10 |
| 151 | B | 20-35 |
| 152 | T | 25-35 |
| 152 | B | 8-10 |
| 153 | T | 8-12 |
| 153 | B | 35-50 |
| 154 | T | 2-10 |
| 154 | C | 15-20 |
| 154 | B | 2-4 |
| 155 | T | 60-75 |
| 155 | B | 3-10 |
| 156 | T | 15-80 |
| 156 | B | 2-10. The signed Spratling 40-55. |
| 157 | T | 200-250 for the smaller one; 600 and up for the large |
| 157 | B | 35-100 |
| 159 | B | 10-22; the larger center one 60-75 |
| 159 | T | 2-15 |
| 160 | T | 18-25 |
| 160 | B | 2-8 |

# BUTTON, BUTTON INDEX